MW01120123

MANIFESTATION

519-ELRO

MANIFESTATION

*Conversations With
Archangel Michael*

Michael El Nour

519-ELRO

Copyright © 2000 by Michael El Nour.

Library of Congress Number: 00-191919

Softcover ISBN: 0-7388-3466-1

All rights reserved. No part of this book may be reproduced or transmitted in any form or by any means, electronic or mechanical, including photocopying, recording, or by any information storage and retrieval system, without permission in writing from the copyright owner.

This book was printed in the United States of America.

To order additional copies of this book, contact:
Xlibris Corporation
1-888-7-XLIBRIS
www.Xlibris.com
Orders@Xlibris.com

THIS BOOK IS DEDICATED TO THE INFINITE CONSCIOUSNESS,
TO ALL BEINGS DANCING AS ONE
IN THE BEAUTIFUL CONCERT OF CREATION.

IT IS DEDICATED TO ALL SEEKERS,
READY TO UNCOVER THEIR OWN TRUTH,
THEIR OWN DIVINITY, ON THE PATH OF LOVE,
COMPASSION AND SERVICE.

WITH MY DEEP LOVE AND GRATITUDE
TO MY SON, MY DAUGHTER,
WHO HAVE ACCEPTED THE CHALLENGE OF SUPPORTING
THE RE-BIRTH OF AN ARCHANGEL
AND TO SHARON L.
WHO HAS BEEN PATIENTLY EDITING MY ENGLISH
FOR MANY YEARS.

Michael El Nour

CONTENTS

SECTION II
PRINCIPLES OF MANIFESTATION

SECTION III
HEAVEN ON EARTH

SECTION IV
LACK OF INTEGRATION

SECTION V
TECHNIQUES

CONCLUSION

FOREWORD

I sometimes wonder about writing. Not only is the market flooded with new books but, most importantly, we have all the answers, within us. We just need to ask our Soul, our God and to listen. So, why would I continue to write?

We are not only Brothers and Sisters. We are One, only one extraordinary body. Also, we are also the multiple facets of God, each of us reflecting a part of His immense Being. The writer the musician, the painter, in one word, the 'Artist' uses this mysterious gift, the gift of communication, the capacity to illuminate, to enliven the threads of Love, which unite individuals and connect them. When one visits a gallery or a museum, one feels Renoir or Van Gogh's personalities, soul, beauty. The **heart** is touched. Love is expressing itself. Listen to a beautiful piece of music and you will dance. Love moves the body. Read a forgotten though, sense it, alive under the writer's pen, and you will participate in the other's vision, the other's spirit, in Spirit. God expresses Himself through Creation, through each and all of us. He speaks to us and tells his secrets, his feeling of beauty. Through an **art** piece, created and then shown, we instantaneously are in **communion** with one another. We hear each other; we love each other.

In this book, I will relate an **experience**. I attempted this for myself, my friends and for all those who are still learning about creation and **manifestation** in the physical world. A human being, in a body, is a product of God's manifestation, but this manifestation is still incomplete unless, we, as human beings also become creators. I started to intentionally use the word MANIFESTATION in 1997. The following pages will illustrate the way our Soul, Heaven and God look at situations. We sometimes think that we know what is good for us, or we imagine our destiny and evolution. But God and the Masters have their own purpose and true manifestation is simply surrender, to be part of the Divine Will on Earth, servants of the Universal purpose.

We are only the **replica of a thought, God's thought.** God is the essence, the origin. He projected Himself onto the feminine substance, the materia prima. After millions of years, we are now the conjugation of two thoughts and frequencies, the divine, original one and our personal signature. Our duty is to **understand God's movement as the Creator and to reproduce it.** We will then be, in the image of God, Co-creators. Why do we speak about Co-Creation? Because we are Whole with God, ONE with His Spirit. It is then impossible to dissociate ourselves from God's existence, life, and breath. However, in order to vibrate and work in harmony, we have to discover how to be One with the Divine.

The main purpose of **information** is not to educate but to **trigger** reactions. Techniques are offered, based on sacred geometry. Any mental/spiritual exercise has several goals:
-To help you see and **manipulate** the **energies**
-To **build** your own **structure** in accordance, synergy with the movement or evolution of the planet and the cosmos.
-To transmute your frequencies progressively in order to become, to **BE** a bearer of the **Christ Vibration** and to help implanting it on the planet.

I would like to insist about an important matter: reading a book is not enough. One does not practice yoga by watching a course, once a month on television. In order to change your level of consciousness, to receive higher initiations, the disciple has to apply the principles that he feels in resonance with to his own life. Applying principles does not take any time. It is a matter of **awareness, conscious self-introspection leading to freedom.** Techniques require practice, like Yoga or Tai Chi. I present them to you in a specific order, leading the practicing reader to a unique result. This cannot be achieved in 10 minutes. In other words, even Christ and Buddha had to work in order to evolve. The Hierarchies are actively guiding humankind and you have your share to do, starting with taking responsibility for your own growth.

A large section of this manuscript was written in 1997, but a major transition occurred in my life, the conscious anchoring of Lord Michael's essence in my physical body, as described in the chapter "SURRENDER". The process that I went through, the questions asked during my birthing process form the body of this book. I believe that **HUNDREDS OF YOU WILL UNDERGO A SIMILAR EXPERIENCE IN THE NEAR FUTURE.** That is the reason why I made the decision to finish and publish the following story.

Also, some parts of this book are still a dialogue between Archangel Michael and Michael, because it happened in this manner. However, this dichotomy does not exist any more, as I AM Archangel Michael . . .

******

MULTI DIMENSIONS, MULTI REALITIES

To understand the phenomenon of multi-dimensionality is to comprehend the true, profound **nature of the Sovereign Creator** of the Universe. I need to make a stop here to explain the terms that I choose to employ. The simple word God is often related, in one's mind with the Judeo Christian god. I find this to be limited and limiting. All the terms found in the human vocabulary related to God are the vehicle of one aspect of the Divine manifestation. The Great Architect of the Universe, Universal Consciousness . . .

"All in One", or "Father/Mother God" and "All That Is" are very appropriate expressions for the period we are in. The principle of multi-dimensions is about to be pierced, not only because of the evolution of human consciousness, but also because of the expansion and affirmation of this principle in the universe itself. In fact, the Universes themselves are in constant evolution. We are an active part of the transformation of a tiny portion of this giant on which we live. It is the transformation and the evolution of the Universe toward more sophisticated structures, de-multiplied, that we perceive, and that allow us, through alignment or natural symbiosis to access to the realization and the consciousness of our own multi-dimensionality.

If we remember that we are a minuscule reproduction of the Whole, it is easy to imagine that we evolve in unison and in the same direction as the Whole and as the Universe does.

Each divine spark emerging out of the Universal Consciousness' womb separated itself from the Whole and fragmented itself in many bodies and universes. (I am simplifying to make this message available to everyone).

Let us use the example of a Soul called Lucile or 'Little Light' (See Illustration). Lucile will create for herself multiple and simultaneous experiences, in **various bodies**, for instance in China, in the United States, in Africa. Lucile might also be alive in different areas of the universe, as a non-human entity, let us say an extra terrestrial on the Pleiades, Venus or Sirius.

We also know that time does not exist, or is only a concept that allows us to mentally explain our existence in the hologram of the 3rd dimension. Thus, what we sometimes call past lives are only parallel lives in **parallel dimensions**. And of course, our **structure** as a human being is also multi-dimensional as the physical, astral, mental and spiritual bodies all vibrate at a different frequency.

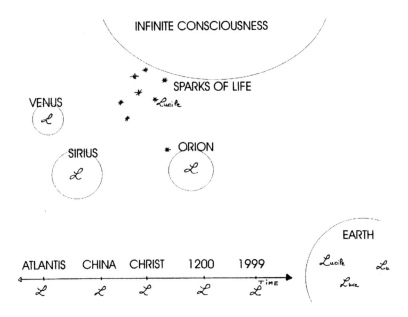

IMPORTANCE OF COMPREHENDING THE MULTI-DIMENSIONAL ASPECT OF LIFE

The true raison d'être of the individual is to remember his origin, his divine identity and to reintegrate himself back into WHOLENESS.

In order to merge again with the Divine Consciousness, the Being must first com-prehend who he is, not only with his mind, but also by the com-prehension of the Self. This means full consciousness at all levels of his existence including the capacity to unify them. When one has truly stopped his state of separation and fragmentation, he will be able to re-constitute or access his divine nature. This process would still take several millenniums, if we were not receiving a formidable influx created by the current evolution of the Earth and the cosmos. If we make the decision to grow NOW and at an accelerated speed, we will receive the de-multiplied assistance and blessings of the Masters and Spiritual Beings who are working in concert with the Cosmic evolution. Words, books and exercises, are not just intellectual games, but working tools designed to bring a specific frequency, to serve our human brothers and the Hierarchies.

To facilitate the access to your multi-dimensions, you have to start by refining your capacities to communicate. **TOTAL COMMUNICATION**, in **UNITY** and **ONENESS** is:

SELF CONSCIOUSNESS/COMMUNICATION

- Consciousness and inner-communication of the Being with himself, that is to say with the **different layers** of this total **structure**, from the physical level to the spiritual.

For instance:
- Differentiation between the state of dream, the astral and the spiritual travel. Also, capacity to use vivid dreams.
- Ability to travel inter-dimensionally and consciously, in and beyond the astral, mental and spiritual frequencies.

- Access and integration of all phenomenon connected to the subconscious mind and clearing of any dysfunction related to it.

- Awareness and communication with the multiple division and extensions of the soul.

- Connection and communication with the Monad. The MONAD is the divine part of the self, or Merged Soul, reconciled with the Whole.

COMMUNICATION WITH OTHERS

The subtle bodies and the sensations of the initiates are refined to the point of complete **empathy** with others. The initiate communicates completely, naturally and at will, from aura to aura.

There is no more need to cheat, be hypocritical, show off or look good, because you have all become transparent, face to face with each other.

You are thus participating in each other's lives; you are healing and balancing each other naturally.

You fully welcome any experience as a group one, knowing that the whole community will be affected. Each challenge is considered as a step forward for the community, endured by and for all, in order to grow and improve the Whole.

When finally you reach Oneness in unconditional Love and compassion, separation ceases to exist. Any creature is a part, a reflection and a flowing expression of God's love manifested before us. Namasté-I honor the God in you-is truly felt and experienced.

SECTION I

I DREAM THE PATH

CHAKRA # 1 — MULADHARA

I LIVE THROUGH INSTINCT

The very first discovery of a soul incarnating on the planet, in matter, is the presence of a **body**. A newborn baby experiences a paradox at birth. He is, for the first time, cut from the constant and comforting presence of the mother and has to start a solitary journey. But simultaneously, he enters a world full of other beings with which he begins an ongoing relationship, an inter-action.

The first chakra contains all of your **vital force**, your life potential. This energy belongs to you; it is a gift, offered by the Holy Spirit and by your parents. Your vital force holds your genetics, family heredity and all the potentialities that you might explore in the life that you are now starting. Any living being, human or not, receives the primal instinct of life and survival. The opening of the first chakra reveals your attitude towards life, your love of life, the way you participate in the activities and joys of the community.

Nobody can elude the gift of life. Even the most suicidal people are fighting and wondering, because the desire to die is in opposition to the magnificent vital force transplanted in the body by the universe.

Your first lesson is then to simply **accept the gift of life** as a miracle and as a present. No struggle is needed to be alive, you are alive. You do not have to do or take anything to stay healthy. Your body knows how to balance itself in perfection. As soon as you surrender to the presence of the Universe and of Mother Earth, you will be nurtured and protected. No one, except you, can separate yourselves from all the blessings offered continuously and without condition to all of the children of the Cosmos and of God.

It is not even necessary to feed your body with material food, but you must treat it with respect and view it as a precious temple. Some of you, because of a troubled childhood, have the unfortunate habit of considering life as a constant fight for survival. Through your subconscious mind, you are sending conflicting messages to your body. One is a desperate cry for survival: "I have to make it, let's do this or that, let's be tough". The second one is: "life is not worth..." In both cases, the body registers a suicidal vibration, a weakness, and translates it as a constant frailty of the immune system leading to chronic illness. Such individuals' lives are loaded with drama that even the most imaginative writer would have difficulty inventing!

Loving life means considering each moment as an opportunity to discover something, experience an emotion, try a new game, visit a friend, start or complete a masterpiece, play, admire a bird or smile at the innocence of a toddler. And when you are challenged, it is only a lesson, a time to demonstrate your wisdom and mastery of life. Or it is an indication that you have to move in a different direction.

To be alive is to be in the **PRESENT** mode. The past, as we will explain later, may be used as a treasure. But nothing is more valuable than the present. What can I do today to make myself feel happy? Do I have food or friends, TODAY? Do I have a roof, a career today? Did I take on my responsibilities, carry out my daily tasks with joy and love, did I kiss my family this morning?

Did I solve my problems and calm any anger that I might have felt? It is important to appease any grievance before going to sleep, to send a thought of love and peace to your family, neighbors and especially to your enemies, if you unfortunately have some.

To honor life is to look around you and recognize the beauty of nature, of others; it is to be able to marvel at a child, a flower, and a sunset. Life is an everlasting miracle: a tiny seed floating around in the wind will find an ounce of soil, root itself and blossom. You have the same ability to find a nest, a fertile ground to grow. However, the plant will not stay alive without roots, sun and light, in other words, without being connected with the environment. In the same way, within our life, you have to develop an intimate connection with the planet, the cosmos, others.

All human beings share the same vital force, although you express it according to your personal note. As soon as you booked your journey to the earth, you signed up for a family, with whom you share emotions and deep connections.

Your **memories** are recorded in your first chakra. As the recipient of the Kundalini Serpent, it is an emanation of your genetics, of your DNA. If one would read your first center, he would know all about your past/parallel existences, the planets that you visited, your karma, your tendencies, etc.

In Muladhara, it is possible to read part of mankind's story, how life manifested itself through the four realms, for instance how the minerals felt when the earth warmed up or shook. What did the plants feel when they emerged from the womb of the mother? Or what a flower or an Amazonian tree feels? Your first chakra could tell the stories of the creation of animals, their instincts, their fears, and their power. Then, you would get familiar with the whole story of the human race, up till now. What an incredible adventure! And finally, the Infinite Consciousness fathered the magnificent creature that you are now, more evolved and sophisticated every day, what a masterpiece!

Life, as incarnated in the **first center**, is **instinctual** life, almost animal. For a long time, in Lemuria and before, human beings had a quite different physical aspect. Closer to the race of the dinosaurs, man had one eye and often lived underground, in the planet's bowels. Man was connected to the spiritual planes but was not fully individualized. He could not evaluate, discriminate or analyze the experiences he was going through. His relationship with the divine force was as instinctual as his contacts with the earth elements, the wind, and the storm. His contacts with other humans were limited to the tribe. The clan existed for the sake of protection and survival.

When you call upon the resources of your first center, you communicate with the will to live as well as the primitive sense of fear and the search for survival. You also have a glimpse at the wildness of all the powerful elements that have come together to generate the apparition of our race. Life on planet earth is a combination of transplants orchestrated by extra-terrestrial beings. Human are a breed; their DNA is a cross between several races. You probably know about the dinosaurs, the insects, the birds and the reptiles.

The first center was considerably modified when the reptiles acquired supremacy on the planet. The reptiles introduced the serpent base energy as well as the ability to discriminate. Humans have been learning through living lessons, choices made by the use of the mind. Wisdom was then a consequence of experience, a path that was necessary for humankind. Now, wisdom is to surrender to feelings, intuition, to God Himself, with complete trust.

To meditate on Muladhara is to be in communication with the archives of the race, the inner part of mother earth, the elements, the semi-intelligent devas who build and keep the form in nature, plants and in the minerals. To dive into Muladhara is to dive into the culture medium of seething life, but with no intelligence.

Astral life forms, tribal ceremonies from Africa or Hawaii, Shamanism, black magic are seated in and are a call to the resources and vibration offered by Muladhara. This vibration is the scream of triumphant, powerful life that can also become destructive when misused or uncontrolled.

Heavy, syncopal rhythm, low bases have the power to wake up the forces of the first center as well as the dormant Serpent. All the dances based on pelvic activation, with the legs—in which the kidney meridian runs-activating the connection with the soil, the nature, are a mean of communication with the terrestrial devas.

Later in the evolution of the race, the Divine fire of Spirit descended on the human race and brought the qualities or vibrations of comprehension and discrimination. Those qualities, when balanced and integrated, generate a perfected mental body. At which times, the individual experiences the sphere of the heart. Those two fires (or forces or principles), mind infused with heart, raise the vibration of the being from the animal nature to the hu-man nature or God-Man.

TRANSMUTATION OF MULADHARA

In order to sacralize the first chakra, one has to bring the seeds of the fourth and sixth centers into it: The divine fire of Spirit, descended on a human being, through the integration of the qualities of comprehension and discrimination. Then, associated with the light of the heart, it raises the vibrations of the being from the animal life to human nature. The human being develops into a restored god by the addition of the seeds of Spirit and of the Heart. The ancestral forces of the low astral have no more power on him. When a human being wants to summon these forces and to communicate with them, using his body, movement and dance, then he infuses them with divine fire and grace. This is the secret of the beauty of the initiate's physical expression. An initiate is no longer a newborn, abandoned by his mother, facing fear, anguish and instinctual survival. He is simultaneously the Father and the Mother, mature, loving, responsible, and magnificent. The initiate is a conscious receptor of God's gift. He is a Co-Creator of the Whole that is to say of the combined masculine and feminine forces in his own structure. The initiate has REPEATED THE ORIGIN, he is in the image of God, HE IS GOD.

Let us use the example of the Sufis. When the dervishes are turning, they do merge the energies of the lower and higher chakras. This is the reason why we discern so much beauty and purity when they are dancing. In fact, to achieve a complete union between Heaven and Earth, they utilize much more than the seven chakras system. They anchor themselves in the Earth and in Heaven and become a bridge.

POINT OF VIEW

One of the most important principles that you need to apply to your daily life is "the art of choosing your point of view".

When you are confronted with any event, situation, when we look at someone else's face or personality, or whatever we are doing, there are two ways to consider life, one positive and one negative.

A situation, as dramatic and difficult as it may seem, always has a raison d'être, that will enrich, transform us and bring us joy. You only need to be open to it and the explanation, the key will be given to you.

Two examples:

-New job or career: Few individuals would accept with joy the sudden announcement of a termination. However, it is an opportunity to find a better job and nicer colleagues.

-End of relationship: Your mate is leaving you or you decide to stop the relationship. If you could look at the situation as an opportunity, you would most certainly meet a more loving, more suitable partner for the new you.

When events and situations are getting spicy, go for a walk, breath, meditate, treat yourself to a good dinner. Then, ask yourself: where is the gift in the story? How can I use this free time? Why do I need to have a vacation?

CHAKRA # 2—SVADHISTHANA

I EXIST THROUGH THE OTHER, INTERACTION

The practice on the second center, SVADHISTHANA, connected with the genitals and to pro-creation, teaches you how to create in the third dimension, while applying the principles of duality. Generally, you experience two phases or stages, the animal stage and the human stage. Then, when you are finally vibrating at the Divine Frequency, in tune with our Divine Blue Print, you manifest, out/free from duality. This is the Divine stage.

ANIMAL STAGE

The second chakra is a lesson about your body, at times when you feel and react mainly through your instincts. Nothing gets us closer to your animal nature than sex, childbirth and anger. Most human beings are still essentially controlled by their sexuality. Passion generates most dramas, crimes and violence. You still have difficulties staying objective when your sexual nature is at work; you forget rules, religion and jump, with both feet in and head first into the most delicate situations, don't you.

This center teaches you the importance of being complete, to hold within your structure both polarities, merged. When a man and a woman come together, they feel happy, accomplished because they feel complete. Then, their meeting makes a creation possible.

They comprehend and express, by the animal and subconscious experience, that creation, of a divine nature, is only possible when the two polarities male and female or positive and negative are in harmony. A couple experiencing the mystery and joy of creation come closer to God and is initiated into the bliss felt in front of any new born or any innocent little cub.

In the organized universe, creation and life are:
-Natural, almost uncontrollable.
-Possible with the harmony and merging of polarities.
-Generate pleasure, joy and a feeling of realization.

HUMAN STAGE

As soon as the race started to evolve, the being felt that brutal coitus, or instinctual inter-action of the forces of nature was not enough. When Spirit and then the Soul were implanted in the aura and in the body, the human being understood the necessity to

- Stop being controlled by his urges
- Add an emotional component to his relationships
- Add discrimination to sexual activity.

Through the search for the significant other, the being discovers many facets of his personality, such as strength, fervor, and capacity to express himself, to create and also to love. The **BODY** is the INSTRUMENT GUIDING US TO THE **POWER OF CREATION** AND TO **EMOTIONS**.

The second chakra is a lesson about **relationships**, practiced like nature, that is to say without thinking, without plan. The natural life force expresses itself through need, impulse, automatism, passion, and love. The sexual glands, connected to the second chakra react to beauty, form, touch and smell. It is often difficult to understand, to logically explain the attractiveness that we feel for another being. The body plays its most subtle card, the awakening of the senses. Beauty has no real criteria; it is a subjective instinctual, sensuous, physical reaction. Suddenly you might meet someone and feel that he/she incarnates beauty and charm. Then, you desire to share, touch, and mix your-selves chemically with this person. Whether it is a hetero or homo-sexual relationship, you think that you have found your perfect comple-ment. SEXUALITY WAKES UP YOUR INNER SENSE OF **COMPLETENESS** and teaches the journey to **DIVINE LOVE,** that only exists when you are complete.

During the human stage, the being is thus learning about emo-tions. Then, comes a time when he desires to give a form, give life to his emotions, through art. This aspect is about the transfer of the energy of the second center to the fifth. The chapter about the throat chakra will then complete this one.

When the being passes the stage of pro-creation and turns into an artist, he then works with the same elements, although applied to objects, projected to his universe. The artist feels:

- Innate sense of an obligation, internal driving force to actually create.
- Utilization of harmony in color, form, sounds.
- Pleasure and joy while working and when the piece is com-pleted.

Finally, the body is a bridge to Wholeness, to the Divine. After the stage of co-dependency, you have a taste of UNITY. You start feeling the desire to be complete, to unite, within ourselves, the two polarities. Then a second step takes place, the discovery that you be-long to the Whole. When you cease to feel alone, separated, you recover your link to the universal body.

CHASTITY and TANTRA

In the past, the candidate to a mystery school, an ashram, would often take a temporary vow of chastity or abstinence. This does not mean that being sexual is opposed to one's spiritual life or evolution. But excess and surrender to compulsions lead us into attitudes and situations that are hurting us later on, because they are inimical to the divine feelings imprinted deep inside us. What is important is the capacity to recognize your desires and master them if they are in opposition with your personal, intimate beliefs or if they are going to create sorrow, violence and chaos.

Mastery of all the negative tendencies, addictions connected with your **physical nature**, are the first step to spiritual realization. It is much easier to hear the subtle voice of the soul when the body stops screaming.

Technically, you have to transfer your basic energy, your attention from the lower to the upper chakras, to the seat of the Divine Self and of the monadic consciousness. Most individuals cannot accomplish this unless they voluntarily and at least temporarily repress their primary instincts—hunger and sex. While practicing spiritually, visualize the energy raising and staying positioned in the heart. Or, pass completely up the spine, beyond the head, and connect with the cosmos.

TANTRA

All of human experience has been based on duality; therefore any aspect of your third dimensional experience has two facets. Sexuality can be purely physical or spiritually oriented. If it is controlled by the will, then by the soul, sexuality may become a bridge to the cosmos and to universal creation.

Tantra is the use of will and visualization to move the energy at the same time that one is engaged in sexual activity. An input on the physical body, in this case the stimulation of the sexual organs, the glands, in synergy with the chakra system, triggers a movement of the universal energy. **Kundalinic** and **Tantric** techniques, when truly practiced can place the lovers in resonance with the cosmos and give them multi-dimensional orgasm. Also, for thousand of years, the body has been the recipient of codes that are just waiting to be activated. The codes, imprints related to Tantra remind us about completeness and wholeness. However, sex, spiritual techniques, movements, yoga, breathing exercises, and contact with a specific energy through a person, a site or an object, toning are only tools to access our memories and activate them.

Although I am speaking to you Beloved, with my heart and in full compassion, I would like to deliver the following important messages:

-It is sad to witness groups, gurus or schools causing confusion in the disciples' minds and hearts. Tantra is not a passport for permissiveness and promiscuity. Whoever tries to control or deal with others through the channel of the second chakra, under the mask or the business card of a teacher or healer is still dealing with his/her lower personality.

-The Divine frequency is definitely established from and above the heart center. It is reached with full merging of matter and spirit and alchemical transmutation of the Self. When one is working towards completeness, he/she will feel less and less desire for bondage, a link with another. And when, Beloved Ones, you merge matter/female and spirit/male inside of you, you feel complete, you are part of the Whole, in full unity, in bliss and adoration, and as such, ARE the pure essence of Love and share yourself with the Whole. Any other being is a part of you. You do not need to be connected with others because you already ARE (God and Whole). And, Dear Ones, you no longer need to express yourself through the human channels of the second and third center. In bold words, sex is becoming obsolete. Sex is attaching you to this planet, as a physical body. Sexuality is what attracted numbers of great Beings into matter, into density. And ascension is the step out of density.

In other words, true ecstasy, Unity and bliss are in God, and God only. Detached adoration of the Divine is possible when one merges, within the Self, the male and female principles, Spirit and Matter, which means when one is complete, out of duality, out of time, out of the bodily experience and of illusion. When one fully surrenders to the Divine, is in Love with the Divine, in love with himself as the Divine and in love with this state of Being, he has moved out of duality, out of the concerns of matter. Then he lets go of anything that might attach him/her to this level of existence. Sex, marriage, family, money are the main components of this human 3rd dimensional organization that you belong to, Dear Ones or more exactly that you are enacting.

In order to fully reach this unique vibration, you have to let go of any attachment to the games and pleasures related to the physical dimension and thus, the body.

Do not blindfold yourselves, Beloved readers, with tantra and soul mates. These are beautiful expressions of love, but still what we will call, without judgement, without idea of separation, still 3rd dimensional love.

In the past, some of you, were monks or nuns, and experienced being in Love with the Christ or with God. When such a feeling was truly coming from the heart, without contacts with astral entities, without exertion or pressure from the family, the religious organization or from the challenge of being a celibate, then, these dear brothers and sisters were in fact ready for the marriage with the Beloved.

IN CASE OF ABUSE

An enormous part of the population has undergone physical mistreatment such as rape, molestation, and forced or inappropriate promiscuity. This painful phenomenon is not new. It is only being revealed now because:

-   Your perceptions are extending; you are aware of your astral and parallel dimensions, where a lot of this abuse did happen.

- You are remembering about your true nature, about your animal nature. You are opening areas of the human brain that were dormant. You are releasing the habit of banishing from your conscious mind any unacceptable aspects of the shadow, and thus creating blockages and degeneration of the self through the subconscious mind.

- Your perceptions of the unacceptable and of freedom have been considerably evolving. You are starting to understand your shadow to the point of loving it.

- For its own growth, the planet has to cleanse itself from thousands of years of practices that are not in harmony with the Christ, divine consciousness.

Individuals who were sexually betrayed show two opposite reactions/tendencies:

- They are repressed, cannot express freely their sexuality, are frigid or impotent, have no desire, initiate a sexual contact without completing it, and of course do not feel fulfilled or happy. In these cases, the answer of the subconscious mind is refusal, negation of what has hurt him/her.

- They express themselves through excess. Hyper desire, hyper-sensitivity, multi partners, and obsessions. The being recreates the phenomenon of betrayal or pain that he grew in and uses it as food to appease his mixed feelings of deception and anger.

The disciple, if he wants to reach freedom, fulfillment and aware-ness, has to clear the harmful imprints that are cluttering his subcon-scious mind. He needs to remember, at least in general, the traumas that imprinted his memories and clear them by making peace with these experiences. The emotions of powerlessness, lack of confidence, guilt have to be detected and transmuted so that serenity and light associated with detachment can be firmly established in the life of the initiates.

PRINCIPLE OF DUALITY

Although the principle of duality has already disappeared from certain spheres of frequencies, it still has impact on many Light Workers who are anchored in the 3rd dimension.

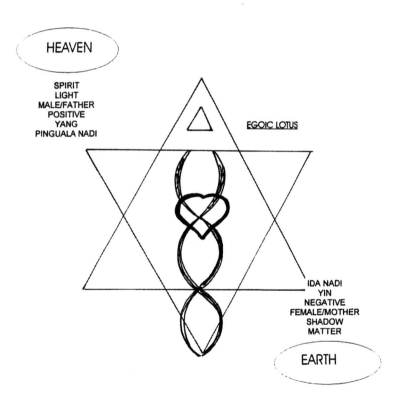

DUALITY - SYMBOLS

HEAVEN

SPIRIT
LIGHT
MALE/FATHER
POSITIVE
YANG
PINGUALA NADI

EGOIC LOTUS

IDA NADI
YIN
NEGATIVE
FEMALE/MOTHER
SHADOW
MATTER

EARTH

THE TRAJECTORY OF KUNDALINI VARIES ACCORDING TO THE BEING

My message to you, Beloved Brothers and Sisters is almost urgent, because your are standing at the turning point of two worlds. Every second brings you closer to the full opening of consciousness of the whole body of humankind. Never has a planet been going so quickly in terms of the enlightenment of a race.

Below the most important points about duality:

The goal of meditation, prayer, yoga, Sufi dancing, in other words of the journey of any incarnated being is to discover the soul and to merge with it, and then to merge with God, the All In One. Before the great marriage, the disciple has to pass several phases:

1. DISCOVERY OF DUALITY
- Comprehension of the nature of life and of the physical body
- Meeting with the shadow, at a personal and universal levels.

2. PROGRESSIVE AND CONSCIOUS TRANSMUTATION

In order to heal himself, the disciple will participate actively:
- Clearing of personal and karmic toxins, in the subconscious mind.
- Creation of a flow of universal energy in the body, powerful enough to support the spiritual work.
- Gradual building and activation of the chakras.
- Discovery of your identity and arousal of the serpent if the DNA allows this initiation.

This process used to be very long; millions of years were needed to build the human creature and thousands for humankind as a group to develop the second and third centers. Along with spiritual evolution, a slow transformation occurs in the DNA and thus at a molecular level. For several years, you have been experiencing an accelerated transmutation that allowed human beings to adjust with the recent changes in the galaxy and the coming of the Christ within each and all of you. In fact, galactic, planetary and human evolution being inter-dependant, the human race is only following the vast ascending movement, which is occurring in this part of the universes. It is then urgent that you accompany that movement and achieve your transformation.

Humankind as well as a portion of the creation throughout the universes made a choice to think in terms of duality.

Duality is connected to the feeling of SEPARATION. The origin of duality goes back to the beginning of times. Although difficult to explain while using terms like time, space, location, bear in mind Dear Ones, that there is no past, no future, no separated space, but only the NOW and the INFINITE.

Imagine a dot, as the origin of the creation. God, or the Vital Principle, or the Universal Love starts thinking and move Himself in space. As soon as he initiates this movement, he is projecting himself and imprinting the infinite with His Presence. In this movement, he also initiates a mirror effect. This is Beloved the very beginning of the re-action, the duplication, of duality. Nothing consciously exists that does not perceive duality. Duality is a consequence of God's will to know Himself through projection/creation.

What is, or more exactly becomes, negative in the duality is the feeling associated with this principle. In your society, based on the precept of good and evil, you have built your awareness on the negative aspect of things and the emotion associated with the separation. Let us explain. If you imagine the creation as an expulsion out of God's womb of fragments of the Divine (souls) starting an exploration journey in the universes, then you might conceive the pain and confusion felt by those souls. But, everything is a question of point of view. Don't you understand the infinite amount of Love expressed, for Himself and for his possible children-you-by God, by allowing you to leave him and much later to come back to him, as adults?

Finally, you are suffering from duality because:
- You live in the human domain, sexually polarized
- You experience the extremes instead of being centered in the heart and divine detachment.

When one reaches wholeness and completion, he is detached from the problems related to duality, even if he is fulfilling his journey in the body.

The notion of good and evil, Light and Shadow, is associated with the following principles:

Spirit	Matter
white	black
light	shadow
positive	negative
yang	yin
male	female
love	hate
trust	fear etc..

Please, look at your hand. It has two faces, but still it is the same hand. Each part has its own raison d'être, and both form a whole, unique and integrated.

In the exact same way, everything in the created universe is polarized with a positive or negative, male or female electric charge. In other words: in the manifested world, and particularly in the terrestrial one, matter manifests itself by the intermediary of two complementary or antagonistic energies that we find everywhere and obviously in the human structure. One energy does not exist without the other and the Whole is Whole only as a marriage, a fusion of both aspects of the creation.

The notion of good and evil was introduced to the soul in order to make possible self-individualization but also to learn discrimination, which is the basic mechanism of the brain.

In order to discover the self, the being needed to see the "other", the non-self, or the reflection of the self in the other. In order to utilize the mind, the plane or the level of awareness that all superior creation has to integrate, the being must learn the choice or binary method of thinking—please note the synonym of thought is reflection, which also means image. The mind reflects or creates an image.

Nevertheless, now, times have changed, literally. Your planet, Beloved, entered the fourth dimension, and you are at the point, as a group, to penetrate the fifth, a world that has nothing to do with anything that you already know. SEPARATION IS DISAPPEARING. TIME and SPACE, as you perceive them, are ABOLISHED. When one ceases to feel alone, abandoned, separated, he rediscovers his real link, the Monad, with the unique universal body. All the laws, principles, scientific as well as moral, are revised. Why? Precisely because duality vanishes to be replaced by the uninterrupted vital flow, the river of unconditional love, the unrestricted sharing.

In order for you Beloved, to get rid of the miasms connected to the duality, I am asking you to modify the feelings and thoughts that you are entertaining every day. Scrutinize your emotions so that you shall change the tissue of your emotional body. This work will progressively affect your physical body, your health and finally your entire frequency.

Below are some of the feelings associated with:

Spirit/Light Matter/darkness

Unconditional love	hatred, despise, condescendence
Trust	fear
Flow	obstruction
Perfection	challenges
Construction	destruction
Letting go	resentment
Allowing/respect	power struggle
Self love. Self-confidence	low self esteem etc

Of course, keep in mind that any aspect of the self is in itself positive and negative. For instance, will might manifest itself as perseverance or stubbornness. Emotional love might lead to weakness and the desire to avoid fear might mask a need for challenge. Any action or behavior might trigger opposite consequences, depending of the point of view of the observers, and of their belief system. For instance, to passionately love animals might entice someone to imprison them in a cage or to respect them.

In fact, and we will speak about this in the next chapters, the most important rule, if we can use this limited term, is to cultivate non-judgement and compassion for the self and for others. Your goal is to jump from a third dimensional, dualistic point of view to the universal principles:

- ALL IS ONE and ONE IS ALL
- NOW only IS, into stillness
- LOVE is the only currency of exchange/relationship.

CHAKRA # 3—MANIPURA

I EXIST THROUGH POWER, IN A GROUP

MANIPURA is about the establishment of one's personality in a society. The being discovers the wheels of life in a group, develops a sense of power—or submissiveness. The feelings of self-confidence, self-love, power, control, abuse are all rooted in the third center.

In this chapter we will only look at certain aspects of your terrestrial journey, and will start with your position in humankind, with your **STORY**.

You all belong to a spiritual family, then to a group soul. The **FAMILY** is the group of individuals with whom you signed deals. For specific reasons, connected to history, heredity or spiritual filiation, you are all associated with the unfolding and conclusion of a story, on the planet or in the galaxy, or even further.

I am not speaking here about fortuitous encounters, about past/parallel lives that might have generated karmic relationships with people that we like or dislike, Dear Ones. We are referring, Beloved Ones, to those who incarnated with a precise goal and who made a vow, with a team, to complete their mission. These individuals are connected with a circle of others that will thus be karmatically affected by the FAMILY.

Think about the term "to **remember**'".

-   It suggests the re-collection of facts, forgotten situations, and qualities that you are. Re-membering is to find the members of your own circle, your own team, to complete the story, your common story and be Whole.
-   It is also the coming together of the different parts of the self until you remember and ARE your Divine Self.

I will use my own story as an example:

"Millions of years ago, a council with origins on the planet Sirius, sent a handful of beings to the Earth, in a capsule. Their purpose was to implant humankind with the genes or DNA of the Sirian race. Besides the genetic implantation they were to bring the Sirian wisdom and culture. They used the Egyptian civilization as the channel to carry the knowledge and the frequency that they were representing. This group worked at the creation of the mystery schools and as a team with Archangel Michael, El Morya and other Beings, I made a commitment to carry my mission up to the turn of the century, overshadowing and balancing schools of initiation. This role/story was linked to the work of the Hierarchy established by Sanat Kumara. In this context, I achieved my work in 1997."

It is easy to imagine that the characters involved in this story will meet, collaborate and eventually compete. They will be incarnating in different areas on the globe and in the galaxy. Each, through personal choices will cause interference into each other's lives. The strongest will help those who weaken, or even abandon the journey. Across the centuries, the members of the team will all have complicated the story with their own experiences, marriages, and children. At a galactic level, the decisions or interests of inter-planetary councils will affect the group, the evolution of the race, the hierarchies' changes and the High Masters' lives.

It is not possible to think that a positive and determined attitude is enough to change, in a glimpse, the decisions, oath, plans, set out millions or at least thousands of years ago, to guide the growth of the planet. The more conscious you are of the complexity of the stories that bond human beings, outer planets, galactic and cosmic systems, the more humble you are. Although the brain and human structure are beautifully sophisticated and powerful, as long as one is not re-united in God, as God, his vision and thus actions will still be ego based or limited. It is then necessary to cultivate humility and surren-der to the limitless, omniscient Universal God. The more capable you are of accepting to be an instrument in service to the Universal Mind and Consciousness, the easier and more successful your path will be.

FORGETTING WHO YOU ARE

This problem affects especially the elder souls, because, behind their human costume, they drag a subconscious mind packed with diverse and often painful impressions and emotions. Often, these individuals with extraordinary gifts have completely forgotten who they are, their origin, their mission, and live, entangled in the web they have built over the centuries. The clothing that they accepted to wear, as a work uniform or a fun disguise became a reality. These Beloved workers are confused about planes and realities Therefore, teammates are sent to them, as rescuers, to wake up their spirits and activate their memo-ries. Messages are transmitted by their souls. Generally, because of the maze that was created by the veterans themselves, very extreme situations or traumas will be necessary to wake them up and bring them back to full consciousness and then to their true mission.

What is the ADVANTAGE, the positive aspect of being AWARE OF YOUR STORY?
- First, you are not alone. Whether you know it or not, you are a part of a huge spiritual family, whose life and interests are linked with yours. You just need to look for them, or to call them telepathically and you will meet them.
- Remembering your true purpose and the big story will give depth to your life. You will be happy to remember, to find the other characters, to help them complete their role. You will

cease to take life too seriously, because the small challenges will have no more impact on you. It will be easier and even fun to accomplish your daily routine, knowing that this is only a play or a mask, under which a very valuable treasure is hiding.

- You will be convinced of your success. Psychologically speaking, it is much easier to believe in yourself and to win the battle when you know that you are teaming with a group of extra-terrestrials originated from the Pleiades, Arcturius or the prestigious lineage of the Melkizedecks.

THE REAL STORY IS HAPPENING
ON THE SUBTLE PLANES

" At age 21, I went through the joy and anguish of a human love story, limitless, unconditional, immense, incomprehensible, and devastating. On the human plane this story turned to a nightmare. I had to pull this man from my life, and I thought from my heart.

Twenty years later, during my long years of healing and remembering, this man reappeared suddenly in my life, in what some call dreams, in fact inter-dimensional travels.

I was transported to a medieval time. From a castle, I was scrutinizing the road, waiting for my Love. He appeared on a horse, tall and beautiful, his long hair waving in the wind. Here he was . . . , and I was still in love with him.

But simultaneously, I was Nora, 1995, and I thought:
"How is that possible, I never think about this man? I questioned the Masters and here was the answer:
"Dear One, this love has lived beyond space and time.
- Why, isn't it such an attachment blocking me?
- No Dear One, it was a protection, a gift, your secret garden. Without this tremendous love around you, you would not have

been able to undergo the challenge that you accepted to carry as part of your spiritual mission."

You are in the habit of considering your physical life as the main part of your existence, as the reality. Dear Ones, you are confusing the movie with reality, the holographic projection of your thoughts and fears with spiritual truth. You have forgotten that your soul, your Monad occupy more space, are more important, more powerful than your dear human bodies, even with such a brain and such an IQ, at times.

If you could read your real story, the one occurring on the subtle planes, you would have fewer difficulties accepting third dimensional challenges. This life that you call real is only a small extension, a child's play, almost a puppet show, projected through the screen of the human mind. Far beyond that, Beloved Readers, a drama of such a dimension and such importance is now taking place, in which you are participating, as the active cells of a titanic spiritual body. You have been living and reliving in your narrow world the interactions of gigantic spiritual beings, encompassing the extension and evolution of a universe, of God's Breath. It is normal for you to accumulate guilt, martyrdom, take things personally, cry for a broken nail, and believe that a lost job or a divorce is the end of the world. But you are just acting as a small bird on a tree or a piece of seaweed dancing at the surface of the ocean. Therefore, act like the birds and seaweed, trust and surrender to God.

My words, at this time:
"If I had known, and could have accepted that my love lived and survived on the subtle planes, if I could have taken the gift instead of crying, my heart would not have been as hurt."
I will add, now, Beloved Readers, that this dream was a glimpse on the multi-dimensional aspect of the self. But my mind was still not capable of imagining or being out of time. Even the answer that I

heard/created from the Beings that I called the Masters was still a reflection of my believe system, of my awareness.

Beloved, your consciousness is still centered in a body that belongs and vibrates in the third dimension. The third dimension expresses itself through codes and habits of matter, through construction and destruction. Money, food and sex are the three axes, the base of this system. You have been conditioned for centuries and thousands of years. Your cells, your astral body are imprinted with the memories of what you call the past, of the gestures and sensations of this linear dimension. It sometimes seems impossible to exist out of this system, without occupying a material function, a mundane or professional life, without eating several times a day and without sexual intercourse. Dear Ones, a regular praying and meditation practice, as a mean of communication and harmony with the Christ Consciousness and the Presence will accustom you, to other vibrations, sensations, needs, other worlds, inhabited by loving, extraordinary beings, your Higher Selves, You.

I AM MICHAEL,
WITH MY DEEP LOVE
I AM THAT I AM.

****

The full process of integration of Spirit on the physical plane might take years. During this journey, do not judge either yourself or the circumstances that you created for your own experience. A lesson is not polarized unless you classify it. A situation is always and only revealing to yourself a different aspect of the Universal Consciousness. It depends on you and you only to make it a success or a drama.

Successive steps of comprehension/vibratory frequencies have to be climbed.
-    You have to understand and feel that something does exist that

is much bigger, much more important than your material life, based on the body, the animal pleasures and power. For some of you Beloved Friends, this is not even a question; nevertheless, your bodies are intoxined with physical habits and programs, that you shall have to get rid of, to transform, in order to affirm, to incarnate the Presence.

- Accept the experience in the body, life in this world, the needs and worries caused by matter. You all choose different paths. For some, discipline and mortification are almost an obligation. For others, Dear Ones, who are not that extreme, a simple daily routine, well rooted in the third dimension will be enough to integrate this stage.

- The disciple often experiences an intermediary stage, that we will call the phase of hesitation. The being feels a stronger and deeper call from his soul and from the Presence. He hears the messages more clearly and uses them more often in his life. He perceives Heaven and the beauty of spiritual reality. As the hiker in a cave, suddenly seeing the light, in the distance, he senses the Spiritual Sun, raises his head and smiles. Eventually, he climbs so high that he experiences momentarily life in the spiritual world. At the beginning, he is a visitor, seated at the feet of the Masters. He is nurtured by their vibrations, their love. Then he meets his true Master, Himself, God in himself.

****

The body, the cells, the DNA are encoded with the memories of the past. What you are dealing with is not your magnificent Self, with the awareness of a Master of a God, but the memories, old desires, old fears. Your mind, your perfect companion and tempter, gives you all kinds of reasons to satisfy your desires. "We need this, it is logical that . . . , our birth right as God's child is". . . well here you are into the mind, fully plugged in the collective subconscious mind, with habits, programs, and you jump right in! Then, because you have already worked a lot, Beloved Ones, you realize: "I am not happier with a Porsche, not even after dating Miss Beverly Hills, making love is not that great . . ."

Well, in that case, why are you so obstinate? Because you are used to living in the drama of the third dimension, because you think that you have to give yourself an appropriate material context as a proof that you have control over your life.

One more word, Dear Friend, to appease you: all the Masters, all the Saints, all of Creation, undergo the same process. There is no challenge that is unknown to them, and yet, they won the challenge of re-membering and re-connecting. Therefore, no self-judgement, no guilt. God loves you, whether or not you feel proud of yourself, unconditionally.

We love YOU immensely.
IN ONENESS.
ARCHANGEL MICHAEL.

****

POSITIVE ASPECT OF POWER

Power, Beloved Readers, has positive aspects that we will now evoke for you. In order to find back his identity and to remember his divineness, a human being has to realize that he owns very rare capabilities. He needs to experiment with his power, his ability to command, to impose his will. He also needs to learn how to organize, create a group structure and have others respect his creation. The human self has to know his space and stabilize himself in it, in full power. If he does not fall into the extremes, such as tyranny, slavery, he is only learning to establish a society, an organization in which individuals cooperate in love and efficiently towards a common goal.

If the energy of the 3rd center is integrated, the being develops an extraordinary physical and magnetic power. He can excel in martial arts and will find all the energy needed concentrated and pure in his Hara. The being recognizes himself, as an individual and affirms himself, while discovering life with others or at the expense of others.

A human being has to learn to be comfortable, in full harmony amongst his kind. This is one of the lessons of the third center. He communicates with others, while realizing who he is. He discovers his capacities and weaknesses, his vulnerability. He will choose to live in the image of the others. Manipura is definitely about image. The two first centers are much more instinctual. Life imposes itself and reproduces. Then the being is interested in himself in the frame of a society. He discovers himself through inter-action and in the eyes of others. Who are the others? What are they doing? What do I feel around others? What do I feel like doing? Following the group, the trends, and the customs? Do I feel stronger, tempted by the position of a leader? Or, do I disappear, because I do not like myself, I feel small, hurt, non-recognized. In the worst situations, the victim frequencies, often caused by traumas in the two first chakras, will anchor themselves strongly in Manipura. Shy, without self-confidence, unable to love yourself, you might hide yourself. In the society, in the power struggle, you will always be aloof and try to become invisible. Faced with anger and strength, you will blush and abdicate. Or after years of silence, you may start on the path of frustration.

Beloved Ones, examine your hearts. Welcome and embrace your sorrow. But please, do not feel any more guilt or powerlessness. We, your oldest brothers, are here for you. We are now here to take your burden. Give your sorrow to us, to God, to the All in One and to your God within. Surrender and let go. Surrender and trust again. Trust God, and you will receive the love that you always looked for.

In the third chakra, the three qualities of vital energies, elaborated in the three terrestrial centers are fusing. These three chakras form the inferior triangle, connecting the Father, the Son and the Holy Spirit, as they appear in creation. The meeting of these three forces animates the dragon, the fire. Then, the dragon raises himself, crosses the heart, the seat of feelings and divine substance. He becomes the Dove. The fire then crosses the three spiritual centers and each of the creative expressions, Father, Son and Action is purified, transmuted and returns to its Divine State.

When the first, second and third center have been transmuted, they are ready to be utilized for full manifestation of the Self, in any dimension. The two triangles, interconnected, are the coming together of the spiritual and the physical self. The two (or more) inter-connected pyramids (or stelleted multi-dimensional figures) are the pattern/symbol of all the parts and forces of the self-united around the core, the divine spark.

In practical terms, the being, when One and Whole, without doubt, without fear, without remains of the untransmuted shadow, is God and creator. The chakras of manifestation in the third dimension are the second and the third, spiritualized or consecrated by God's breath, spirit and Love (love is God's power). These centers root, anchor, in the physical domain, in the body of the individual, the magnificent GodSelf. A thoroughly completed and integrated clearing of the feelings of abuse, inadequacy, self-pity, failure, thus a full acceptance of self, are the basis of manifestation.

The understanding and integration of all the above-mentioned "negative" emotions is in fact the comprehension of the true nature of the shadow. As I already said, the Shadow is nothing more than the opposite of Light. When experienced and merged with the Light, it is simply the tool of God's expression-thus your tool-in the physical or manifested world. I am not expressing that you have to keep these feelings but to recognize the positive aspect of any situation. If you understand and accept to see and feel the good side of your dramas and failures (sensed as), if you bless any new lesson, any enemy as your teacher and are capable of feeding/constructing yourself on the basis of Love and compassion, the shadow as the adversary vanishes and is your friend. You have accomplished the alchemical transmutation and the codes of your DNA are being changed, switched. Daily practice in such a spirit, a state of mind will lead you to full mastery, avatarship and Godness.

BE IMMENSELY BLESSED, DEAR READERS.
MY HEART POURS LOVE AND COMPASSION TO-
WARDS YOU
I AM ONE WITH YOU
I AM ARCHANGEL MICHAEL

Self-compassion, self-love, which automatically induce love and compassion for others, full recognition of the others as self, lead to creation. However, in his act of creation, the Beloved Christed initiate does not rely on himself, in isolation and separation, but as Himself as God, fully surrendered to the All Existing, All Pervading Heart/Mind of the Universes. When one knows and experiences his godly power/ love, dissolution of the ego happens that annihilate the restrictions generated by the frequencies of duality and separation. Consequently, manifestation only IS.

IN LOVE AND COMPASSION
ARCHANGEL MICHAEL.
YOUR SITUATION IN THE WORLD

The third center being the expression of yourself in a group, in the world, I will give you some insight about finding your true self.

The Divine can only reveal itself in the world of manifestation when it is truly welcome and accepted as it IS, as Divine, perfect, all Love and all Power. This is only possible when the Being stops wondering about himself, about his true nature and his true self.

Rooted in your long habit of existence in the illusion of the physical world and of suffering, many of you, Beloved Readers, still do not believe and trust yourself. You still do not fully recognize yourself as an extension of God, and therefore, are not allowing the flow of God's own life force to manifest in your human life.

MORE ABOUT THE SHADOW

As already stated, everything in the universe, whether labeled as positive or negative, can be used for a "good" purpose. It is interesting that when one is living out of duality, all words seem charged and consequently, announcing that something is "good" is already a judgment, but let pass on that and use third dimensional wording.

One way to see the physical chakra system is to divide it in two parts, under and above the heart. The centers number one to three apply to our mastery of matter, of physical values and experiences. The three upper chakras are connecting us with Spirit, with our spiritual self.

In order to achieve completeness, we have to merge Spirit and Matter or Light and Shadow. This fusion occurs when one is no more afraid or judging himself for his expression of the dark side of the universe. It is also important to be educated, aware of the passions, of the extreme frequencies/situations inherent to incarnation and human nature and then to accept these tendencies instead of feeling ashamed, guilty, and dark. Allow any vibration, any experience as a contact, a knowing of God, as ALL IN ONE, ALL IT IS, All pervading and omnipresent.

In order to create, Source had/has to reach, embrace the frequencies of materialization, of matter, of the shadow or reverse side of the Light. In a similar way, we have to understand and use the so-called negative/lower chakras in their positive aspect.

We already spoke about procreation and sacred sexuality as tool to create and awake the serpent power. This is achieved by the blending of polarities. Through the second chakra mother earth, as one with her children, celebrates the power of the feminine, the nurturing, flowing, all giving nature of Life and of God, the ability to welcome, nourish and sustain Creation.

The blooming of the third chakra, for the planet as in human consciousness as a group, is the discovering and enforcement of strength, power, and assertiveness.

The combination of those two vibrations engenders the possibility of all expressions through the merging of the extremes in the heart. In a more concrete way, I would say, Beloved Readers, that instead of denying the lower self, one has to use it to manifest. You have to use your **sanctified shadow as your tool to express yourself in the realm of matter.** I am not advising you to go back to the mean, sex addicted, shark type animal. But, realize that the positive aspects of the lower centers are required to be a Creator.

Let's summarize:

Third chakra:
Self-acceptance, self-recognition, self-empowerment, male/active force, feeling of comfort and ease in the physical world. Strength, ability to stand up for self in integrity.

Second chakra:
Self love, recognition of the beauty and power of the Mother, ability to give/serve without condition-which is the prerequisite to receive, ability to be with the flow of the life force, to surrender to Spirit or male aspect of God when creating. God is not creating by entertaining separation and solitude. God creates through you, for you, as a partner in the material world.

THE NEED TO BE RIGHT AND TO PROVE YOURSELF RIGHT

The need to prove everything or to understand-Cartesian philoso-phy-is rooted in the fear of not being accepted, heard, recognized, or the fear of knowing the truth. It is much easier to convince yourself that a whole lifetime is necessary to search for the truth, than to accept the easy way, the path of the heart and the emotions. How is the heart speaking? Through a twinge, a feeling of joy, of heaviness. This is the language of the soul, of the Divine.

Some of you will spend their whole existence either imprisoned in the past, or scrutinizing books or so-called facts. This planet gave birth to great thinkers, scientists, cabalists and alchemists who are twisting words, letters and chemistry in order to discover the magic formula. But all this is only a distraction, the fear to see the essential, and the core, whose root and key are in the heart.

Just ask yourselves Dear Ones, what are you afraid of? If you are dealing with a specific problem, ask yourself: why do I react with my guts, or with sorrow to this word, to this idea. Why do I need to prove this or that? Do I believe it myself? Is there something very simple or very serious that I do not want to see or to hear?

All the laws, the limits that we accept to join with, whatever pretext we choose, for instance the purity of a religion, are still rules and barriers placed around our world in order to cover the truth, pure, simple and beautiful.

When one feels the need to elaborate logical discourses and proofs to the point of torturing himself as a masochist (and others), he is only:
- Looking for reasons to avoid a reality that he knows but might be too painful to admit as true.
- Too weak or too hurt to change a habit, a belief about the world or about himself in order to enter the path of higher consciousness and freedom.

It is much easier to hold on to an idea or philosophy, or to belong to a system or a religion, with precise rules and demands than to surrender to God Himself. Why? Because one is not necessarily aware of God's will and because God does not give you a program, with a precise schedule and the certainty of a checking account. Because integrity engendered by true love, complete acceptance of others and of the self, moved by discernment, harmony and in the present, requires much more courage than to obey a book, with rules stated by a human leader.

Also, the individual who belongs to the human race, as ONE, as a UNIQUE BODY instead of being a citizen of a country, a member of a sect, does not judge anyone for his race, color, belief or money. Whoever abstains from carrying any human banner is more than tolerant. He is not affected by differences, but recognizes the diversities of the Whole. He loves, without judgement, participates equally, without ambiguity in all of the manifestations of the Divine Presence.

YOU NEED OTHERS'S APPROVAL because you do not have enough faith in your own value and in the value of your own judgement. You are still looking for a mirror in the eyes of others, which would feel more acceptable to you or someone with more compassion than you have for yourself.

NEED TO PROVE WHO I AM
Do I need to demonstrate who I am?
YES, if I do not know who I AM,
NO, if I know that I AM, which means if I have met my divineness and do accept it from the depth of my heart and my soul.

An adult is one who has left childhood behind, whose universe is not limited to his parents' arms. The child only mirrors himself in his parents' or in others' eyes. He does not know the world, because he is too young or because he is afraid of the world. An adult lives outside of his parents' universe. His reference system is enlarged. He no longer needs to be recognized, or acknowledged by his parents or to demonstrate what he is or is not.

At the beginning of the century, families were still living like tribes. From the grand parents to the grand children, each had a specific role, prerogatives, received the honor or attention inherent to his age or wisdom. It was not necessary to leave the clan and create your own world, by yourself, confronting the group, you/your world and the group as the exterior world. In the desire to incarnate and experience the extremes your society created a frame for independence, solitude, away from the community. This lesson also experienced in the political arena, proved itself wrong. The perfect system, the divine one, the one that provides respect and sharing has still not been established, because the countries and leaders are still moved by power instead of unconditional love. We are finally approaching a period favorable to the establishment of a true community, based on osmosis, unity, telepathy, a shared consciousness and One Heart. But in order for this type of society to be instituted, it is necessary that all the members, or at least the leaders have evolved to the point of having passed the ordeal by fire, consciousness, and have been reconciled with themselves and with God.

The currency, the energy flowing in a family or society is
- On the physical plane, food and money.
- On the emotional, human love.
- On the spiritual, divine unconditional love.

The third center, Manipura is connected with adolescence. When a young person lives with his family he has to establish his life in the world. But in order to assume his life and responsibilities, he has to break the small circle of the family. He needs to go and exist, without restrictions, without limits, without frontiers in the infinite world. He then has the ability to share, exchange, live, produce, create the flow with the Whole, in its diversity, and with an infinity of beings.

Below some facets of eternal childhood:

- A wife/mate completely dependent of his/her companion.
- An individual always in need to be rescued, by family, friends
- A homeless person, eventually taken care of by the society
- The monk, refusing the world, who escapes into a monastery or in prayer.
- The genius finding a refuge in the intricacies of his brain, unable to face society or the basics of life: to be clean, to get rest, to feed himself.
- The artist, in communion with some aspect of his soul, living completely out of the system.

CHAKRA # 4—ANAHATA

I AM THROUGH LOVE

Although I will dedicate a full chapter to the hexagram or six-pointed star, I will start this subject now because ANAHATA contains the six-pointed star.

Harmony and equilibrium between the extremes can be read on the human structure horizontally and from the top to the bottom.

Between the right and left sides, the two polarities are balanced. Two meridians, feminine and masculine, two lobes of the brain, etc . The heart, anatomically speaking is an example of fusion, of the potential results expected by the two polarities simultaneous operating. Two ventricles perform the function of the heart. The right ventricle sends the polluted blood in the pulmonary artery where it will be purified. Then, the left ventricle expels the precious liquid, ready to nurture the body. The two parts of the heart as well as the two functions are inter-dependant. The two extremes are moving in a unique beat.

In the terrestrial and multi-dimensional journey, the heart chakra intervenes at two levels.

First, the disciple reaches enough harmony within himself and is free of the dilemmas of the three lower centers. The individual is then dwelling in the fourth chakra, which is the junction, the marriage. He is mid-way between Spirit and Matter and keeps close to the world of feelings and sensations. At this stage in his spiritual life, he will clean his emotional body of the psychological and subconscious barriers that make him unable to express his true emotions. He will also meet his past and make peace with all the emotional scars still noticeable through clairvoyance in the heart chakra.

Then the being will undertake the building of the three upper centers. When these chakras are reaching a reasonable state of opening, through understanding and commitment, the disciple will pass new spiritual initiations and will COME BACK TO BALANCE HIMSELF IN THE HEART CHAKRA. (See Six-Pointed Star, in chapter seven).

******

The five-pointed star or pentagram is a symbol of the incarnated human, who happens to have five main senses, at least in this world. The five senses are the attributes by which the physical body is not only alive, but also participates in the joys of life. Interestingly enough, one can live without physical senses. However, they are the spices of this journey, a preamble to the highest sense, the Whole one, the divine, unconditional tool to communication, LOVE.

As a matter of fact, love whose seed and root is in Anahata, embraces all the other senses and magnifies them.

One enjoys an original, delicate taste . . . one loves . . .

One opens his lungs and smells a perfume . . . one loves

One admires a flower, a sunset, and a face . . . one loves

One listens to a voice, a bird song, a musical piece, one loves

One places his hand or his cheek on another's skin, on the fur of an animal or even a rock . . . one loves . . .

LOVE is the perfected act of communication. It unites all the senses, and does not question. It is the sharing, the interaction that gives rise to joy, contentment, fulfillment, perfect creation.

TRAUMAS OF THE HEART CHAKRA

Several reactions can be expected. Anahata remains closed and the consciousness find refuge in other centers.

1.   The individual might, subconsciously, decide to lock his energy at the level of the third chakra. He will then mainly search for personal power in the physical world. Mundane life, social position, profession will be the goals of his existence. The being will compensate the loss of love, self-love and love for the others, by:
- A breach of his personality, with low self-esteem. In this case, he will create situations to hurt himself, affirm his negative self-judgement and prove that he deserves nothing.
- He will over-demonstrate his capacities and power, in order to attract attention, compliments. Unable to see his own beauty, he will use others as mirrors. Attention will be his food and a crowd, his mirror.

2.   A second response to an emotional trauma is a stabilization of the energy in the sixth center. This kind of reaction appears in individuals who are more cerebral or more evolved. The mercurian type will explain, analyze instead of feeling, of vibrating. Exegesis, debates, and techniques will attract them. Sensitive people will choose the path of intuition or psychic powers, according to their vibration level. A probable battle will occur with pure intuition, this later being linked to their ability to listen to the heart.

3.   The most serious consequence of a wound on Anahata is the difficulty to communicate with the soul, which seats, on the human level, in the heart. Depending of the stage of awareness of

the individual when the trauma takes place, we will witness either a complete inability to connect with the soul or a distortion of the messages expedited by the soul. The erroneous interpretation of the divine missives will depend on the chakra in which the consciousness and the personality are being trapped. The being will then experience all kinds of complex situations by which the soul is trying to be heard.

When an individual is connected with his heart, and surrender to the love vibrations embedded in this center, he is capable of seeing and appreciating himself, as well as to manifest compassion for his humanness and weaknesses. He will look at them as a gift, the capacity to feel, to be in communion with human vicissitudes in the way of the Christ. He understands sorrow and resistance engendered by incarnation, but does not judge. He knows that all of this is temporary, an illusion, integral part of a play but very limited.

****

The heart is a gentle flower unveiling itself to the passer-by, broadcasting an unexpected scent. The heart is the door, the key of all the mysteries.

Who are the masses attracted to? Those who love others and love what they do. The soul, being the spark of God in the human being, can only love. If the heart is open, the others will feel God and naturally respond. Human beings sometimes have difficulties revealing their true self because they feel vulnerable. Therefore, Beloved, some of you are always hesitating in the three first centers.

You cannot wait anymore. You have to love yourself, love Mother Earth and recognize yourself in the Creator God. It is time, Dear Ones, to re-animate the flame, forgotten for such a long time, in order for humankind to rest in the aura of Divine Love and to settle in the heart frequency.

Entire civilizations have been destroyed, races are dying because they could not love, develop feelings. Through the Christ and the Ascended Masters, you have seen the demonstration of the power of love, which gives without judging. You have the duty, Dear Ones, to abandon all the emotions holding you away from the heart, from Love, from God, so that humankind shall be reestablished into peace, health, so that Mother Earth can heal. Compassion is the key for the restoration of all human relationships. It is impossible to criticize, judge and pretend to love God. God is alive in all creatures. Thus, by judging others, you judge yourself as a human as well as yourself as the recipient of the Divine Flame.

In Perfection, Compassion
In Pure Love,
I AM MICHAEL

CHAKRA #5—VISUDDHA

I AM and EXPRESS MYSELF THROUGH CREATION

While the petals of the lotus delicately open and the layers of the spiritual self-blossom, the disciple and then the initiate learn to reproduce the phenomenon of creation and manifestation.

How did the Divine create? Certainly by the powerful influx of His thought but moreover from the wisdom of His BEINGNESS, expressed outside of himself. The first stage of this process is the will to leave momentarily his state of Being to project himself. In order to materialize, God used the word and sound.

Imagine an initiate creating in his domain. He wishes to manifest something, a condition or an object, which would be a source of joy for himself or for someone else. He will think about it, with a feeling of contentment, of peace, with an internal and external smile. Eventually, he will say: "I love this tree, blossoming with so much fruit, or "I would love for my friend Lucie to receive a new car for her birthday". For himself, the message is generally only a brief thought, like this: "It would be agreeable to wear a new green outfit or to manifest the money needed for this project."

This is enough. After emitting this vibration of joy, while thinking about something, completely abandon this idea into the arms of the universe. If one does not surrender, he will block the manifestation. This is the only secret, letting go.

The throat center, when harmoniously functioning, is extremely beautiful and vibrant. Beloved Readers, when the energy of this center reaches out, it touches the world and sends its vibrations with the love and the grace of a flower of Light.

All the centers are organs of communication, but Visuddah, crystallizes the sharing with sounds or the manifestation on the 3rd dimension.

The second chakra is the physical inter-action with potential pro-creation. The third center is the relationship with others, the way you establish and live this relationship. The heart is about feelings. The throat is the center through which the creator will express, not only his human quality, but also his personal note, and he will offer it to others. What is his blueprint?

At the monadic level, Visuddha is completely activated when the Being IS the Presence:

- He/She changes his language to manifest the purity and love emanating from God.

- He uses the sacred words and encoded sounds unveiling in himself and others all the memories, opening all the keys. Each of you, Beloved Ones, is a very special piece of the puzzle, and in order to open, to expand yourself, to be fully realized, you have to be touched. Some may contact God directly, through work and surrender, others will need a meeting with someone, a vibration, a word. Those, who, as the body of the Christ, plant the seeds, naturally accomplish all this by the word of the initiate.

- He only spreads words of grace, with the intent of healing, praising, encouraging, building, loving. He does not speak in vain, but only to express wisdom. Negative talk, criticism, doubt no longer exist, because he is the activated, current keeper of the Presence.

- If he is encoded to express the Presence as a public speaker, or as an artist, his creation will testify of the presence of God and Christ around him. Those who admire or see his art will be touched by I AM and will evolve faster.

- The initiate, in direct communication with God, adjusts his steps, his life, and his activities with the scheme of the Hierarchy. He feels or knows his assignment, and stands with it, in the NOW, living his mission. He creates an extension of the Presence around him, in his small universe. As each bee in a beehive instinctively contributes to the life of the community, the initiate, rid of the veil of the ego and of the personality, offers his energy to the establishment of the divine will in the third dimension where he resides.

****

Visuddha is a bridge. It opens the way to the three centers of the head, which have to work in synergy. It is a bridge because, when its energy is strong enough, Visuddha gives away, yields the command to the Alta Major, the key of the upper triad.

On the cabalistic tree, the Alta Major is situated on the central pillar, at the cross through which the energy raises itself. On the classical sephirotic tree, there is a space between Tipereth and Kether, called the Abyss. It is the space that must be crossed over between the material and the spiritual worlds, between the 3rd and 4th dimension.

Although one category of individuals jumped the abyss alone, through work, patience, endurance, and often tears, the race in general, as a group, has been helped.

In 1997, a comet crossed your system as a precursor of the Aquarian era. The energy brought by Hale Bopp was a gift, a service to the group. A sephiroth is a planet, let us say, a stable manifestation, although all the creation is in fact holographic in essence. A comet is not fixed, with a dense core, it is polarized differently. This explains its exceptional appeal, the fascination of human beings with this phenomenon.

The passage of the comet was concomitant with to the end of the Hierarchy conducted by the Sanat Kumara, and the transition to the 4th dimension. Let us remind you that the Alta Major was the security system which was used by this Hierarchy, to make sure that humans will fully incarnate, in the physical plane and momentarily lose their connection with Heaven, in order to confront matter, the polarities, using the mind and discrimination. This goal, having been reached, the race started then an ascendant movement, to re-conquer Divineness. We could also use the term to remember their Divineness, after the integration of the Conscious Light or Light merged with the shadow.

The planet Daath, which is in the middle of the Abyss is defined in the Cabalistic Encyclopedia" from David Godwin as follow: "Knowledge. Non-sephira, localized in the Abyss, under Cochmah and Binah but above Yesed and Geburah."

The Alta Major is the key, the link, in the physical body, between Heaven and Earth, between the invisible, spiritual spheres and the visible, material ones. On the cosmic level, in the systemic body to which mankind belongs, the link was made by a non-planet, a comet, which brought with itself the vibration of the light and the fusion.

The comet, as the astral chart on January 23, 1997 showed it, brought the vibrations and the holographic picture of the hexagram, or as seen in four dimensions, the star tetrahedron.

Note: planets, systems, galaxies are under the responsibility of spiritual Beings, organized in Hierarchies, according to their level of consciousness and commitment to God. The evolution of a planet or a race is planned and monitored by the Hierarchies.

****

WHAT IS A GIFT, A TALENT

Gifts are the manifestation of the Divine Spirit, of God, through and by a being.

The divine spark, One and Multiple, expresses itself through thousands of pathways. Each being, human or not, each part of the creation, from the insects to the plants, to the gigantic nebulous, is a facet of that Essence, of the Whole.

A gift is a diamond, directly sent to you, by Source, as an expression of the greatness and the beauty of the Creator God.

Each of us is responsible for our gift, the pearl that was delicately enshrined by the universe in the temple of your body. When one has found the pearl awaiting in the heart, he is expected to respect, polish, shine, and give attention to it in order for it to grow. Then the pearl will be revealed to the eyes of your brothers and sisters, the others searchers, the other inhabitants of the beehive. They will discover the pearl, admire it, through their eyes. But moreover, the quality of the pearl, the amount of effort it represents, the intensity of the emotions involved, the flow of passion seeded in this unique piece of jewelry will reach and awaken the heart of the witness, of the visitor, because two souls will have shared an emotion together.

This pearl, offered, is a direct contact with the divine essence. When one responds to the divine influx of creation, he instinctively establishes a bridge, harmony between his vibrations and the divine frequencies. The more detached he is from the social and societal habits to keep himself close to his personal note, the more life Energy will flow through him. This energy will purify him, sculpt him as a perfect channel between Source and the public. The artist is then contributing to the process of healing, of evolution, of harmonization of the planet.

ART AS AN EXPRESSION OF GOD

Why is art so essential? Because the artist, when he is living his passion, is detached from the mental world and connected to his soul, to God. He automatically positions himself in resonance, harmony with the heartbeat of the world and the universal creating flame.

The value of art does not reside in forms or techniques, but in the hidden message. Art reveals the soul. Movement and colors go far beyond the mind, beyond rules and standards, to reach this small vulnerable area in you, this part in you which is so close to the Divine that you might have attempted to hide it. The feeling of joy and harmony felt while listening or looking at a piece of art re-animates, resuscitates this forgotten part or yourself and helps it to express itself again.

Some artists are already blessed as conscious instruments of I AM. As soon as they start playing music, dance or paint, they are the full expression of God. If you are granted the joy and honor to watch them at this moment, you will immediately be in a blissful, meditative state. Through the artist, you are automatically in alignment with your own monad, with the Presence.

Beloved, may God bless you all, for your beauty, for your art, for all the parts of God that you share with the world.
We thank you and love you.

ARCHANGEL MICHAEL,
ARCHANGEL OF THE BLUE LIGHTNING.

CHAKRA #6 — AJNA

I AM ONE WITH THE HOLY SPIRIT.

MERGING THE FORCES OF DUALITY

The sixth chakra is the balancing of the dual forces of nature. The initiate has completed the struggle between the extremes and centered himself in the pool of energy that leads to mastery and belongs to the Master.

Throughout time, the searcher encountered all kinds of situations, which attracted him to one side or the other of what cabalists call the tree of life. He met addictions and passions, but no real quietness and serenity. After the merging, when this magnificent achievement is completed, the new master over matter is no longer challenged by duality experienced through humanness. Both of his channels of energy have been cleansed enough and strengthened in order to be able to welcome the two sides of incarnated nature to come through and establish their kingdom in the Ajna, the 6th, in Oneness. The individual's feelings towards life also change. The greatest joy will not let him be enraptured, while the lessons inherent to life in the 3rd dimension, will be acknowledged but not affect him out of proportion and bring him to deep sorrow, dysbalance and depression.

The 6th is the realization that nothing is possible without merging, without the middle path or path of the Master. In the Ajna, the light and the shadow no longer exist in a differentiated way. They start, per se, a new life as One. Thus, the Christ, the Lord of the Conscious Light, is able to establish his own kingdom, first in the higher structure, and then in the heart of this Beloved One. The Christ comes, dispenses his frequency and another being is ready to embody the Christ Consciousness.

MERGING IN THE HOME OF
THE HOLY SPIRIT

The 6th center is the home of the Holy Spirit. The Holy Spirit was born, to use human words, from the father and mother's marriage, or from the reflection of the Infinite, coming back to Himself. The Holy Spirit is God's arm, extended and manifested, in the creative reality of the world of manifestation.

What is the role of the 6th chakra as a center of manifestation? The energy has to become One, united, in order to be ready to express itself. The re-union into bright light after going through the heart, initiates a new sense of self as well as a new capacity to attune oneself with God's arm or the flow of the Universal life force.

We know that Planet Earth was chosen, for a special purpose, the bringing together of the two energies faster than in other areas of the universe. You, who made a commitment to be a part of this experience, might sometimes wonder how to conceive Self as God, as a tool for God's manifestation. Well, in fact, it is possible to achieve such a relationship with the God within, such a sense of Oneness with the Infinite Consciousness, such a soft feeling of God's presence that surrender and acceptance are natural, ARE. In fact, the Beloved blessed recipient is just transferring God's ability to create or God's state in the 3rd dimension.

The coming together of the forces allows the marriage and the anointing by the Holy Spirit. The marriage, as we already stated it, dear friends, is not only the fusion of the two sides of the energy but also the marriage with the God within. The God within was met, when the disciple journeyed into his heart chakra, and he will go back to the heart. Nevertheless, the inner divine energy is now going to represent itself in manifestation. When Ajna is completely built and seen in clairvoyance, it appears on the forehead of the initiate as two wings or two petals. Supported by the two wings, stands the blue flame of the Holy Spirit. It is the result of the completion, of the new state of the Master, in equilibrium between the columns of fire and action that supported him in matter, gave him form, but also generated emotionally challenging adventures.

Now the being is in contact with the inner God, he is the Monad or at least in communication with his Monad. He hears clearly the divine voice or intuition. This is the reason why the tradition used to speak about the Ajna as the center of intuition and vision.

What about vision? Because the new Master has completed the journey of matter, emerged the winner of the hurdles, he has torn down the veil of illusion that obstructed his vision. Let us bear in mind that, on the tree of life, Ajna is located above and in alignment with Malkut, Maya, and the illusion.

The end of the obstructed vision is marked on the third dimensional plane by the junction of the pituitary and pineal glands, with each other and with the Alta Major center. It is the synergy, the simultaneous action of these three areas, frequencies that create the clear revelation of the inner God and the CAPACITY to LISTEN TO IT.

BEing into quietness, not experiencing the constant traction on one side or the other of the pendulum, allows the new master to introduce a wave of calm and peace into his life. God is sensed, felt, in a new or more subtle way and in freedom, without the necessity to be either or. It is also a time of serenity because the being is not even searching for the blessings dispensed by the Holy Spirit. He knows that everything is available in quietness and that the gifts are within himself. Many gifts are offered, which can be accessed through intuition and through the eye of Horus.

SECRETS OF KNOWLEDGE

Also in the sixth chakra dwell the secrets of knowledge. We do not mean, Beloved Brothers that you are suddenly going to write down Einstein's theory, although it is possible. But the initiate has access to the divine sea, the space or field in which everything exists in potentiality, in waiting for manifestation. Interestingly, in French mother is 'mère' and sea is 'mer', thus homonyms. The father, or Spirit, is the initiator of the movement, bringing to life, fecundating the Mother. Through his work and commitment, the initiate made possible the meeting of the mother and the father. The door is thus open to realization and self-realization. In terms of awareness, the being now KNOWS, intuitively, and discerns through his instinct, for several reasons:

- The initiate hears the voice of the inner God when needed, even before asking a question.

- He is not confused by the illusion of the third dimension, and can now receive information from the higher planes without the distortions connected to the 3rd dimension and the ego.

- He is the sum of the experiences of the past, of the codes situated in his chakras number one through number five. The initiate has re-animated, opened his centers and is now capable of using any information, experience, or emotion that he has gathered, gleaned through centuries of lives and adventures. All this understanding, all these energies fuse into the sixth center when Kundalini arouses and the initiate is now capable of using all these treasures without inhibition.
  In fact, the marriage in the Ajna takes place at different levels:
- Marriage of positive and negative energy (=Light and Shadow)
- Marriage with the Spirit or celestial frequencies that the initiate is now receiving.
- Marriage with the soul and then the Monad.

What is knowledge?

- Self-knowledge, self-awareness
The disciple has spent many years in front of the mirror of life, looking for himself in battles, joys and relationships. He has only been able to reach this level of awareness, because he overcame the fear of recognizing the self in any and every quality, every aspect of the divine nature, any other being. He has had long journeys with his shadow and has learned to love all and every part of self. He is perfectly comfortable and content with what he found out and what he refined. He has been overshadowed by the inner God who sublimes the self to transform it into a part of the Whole, the One.

- Knowledge of the divine laws:
We are not speaking here of a the ability to describe the physical laws of the universe, as a scientist, but to comprehend and apply to the self the spiritual principles that govern the inter-actions between the members of the immense family engendered by the Divine Consciousness. The cognition or intuition of these principles allows the initiate to live in peace with himself and with others. He knows what his natural rights are but also his limits.

For instance, Dear Ones, you speak about free will, thinking that you can make any choice, in the name of it. However, during your numerous existences, you might have understood that the incarnation—condition of being incarnated, caro=flesh—turned you into turbulent children, sometimes stubborn or blind. Often, your choices, based on incomplete information, on fear or past emotions, or on the need to claim your independence, led you to sorrow or defeat. You might have sometimes had the certitude to act in full mastery and intelligence. Nevertheless, after many years, you finally were capable of simply recognizing your weaknesses, your emotional confusion.

Vision and awareness of the divine principles are linked together. Have you noticed how difficult it is to explain some things to a child?

Why? Because a child lives in his own world, limited by his intellectual, emotional, and spiritual faculties, inherent to his age and blueprint. In fact, a lot of adults are incapable of seeing the belief systems or habits that have been blocking their lives all along, holding them away from peace or success. Of course, we are not judging, classifying or separating. From the third dimension it is often difficult to have clear, full vision of the structure and multi-dimensional destiny of a being. Who really knows what the contracts were, the decisions made by the soul in terms of the experiences that they agreed to create on the planet. What are the criteria of beauty, success, happiness for your monad, in the immense diversity created and agreed upon by God Himself?

We will thus say, Beloved, that there is a time where the individual acquires enough clairvoyance combined with enough consciousness to be able to perceive and change his/her behavior, his thoughts and therefore his life.

The principle of non-intervention in one's life is fundamental and part of God's wonderful wisdom. Imagine a story: Master X, once decides to create a collective miracle. All the individuals will suddenly become masters of wisdom and will live according to the Master X model, that is to say in Universe Y, as hermits, asexual, and with a cat as a companion . . . and so on, use your own imagination. Who will really be happy? Who will decide if the world projected out of Master X thoughts is the right path for all of the individuals whom he selected to grant with a miracle?

Let us go back to the sixth chakra. The blossoming of a center does not signify perfection, everything is still relative. Let us say that the being who has developed Ajna has accomplished enough to see this small portion of the universe, which is his world, without the veils of matter, fear, and emotions. In his world, he will receive the flow of wisdom and divine love, and enjoy the perfection of the

Infinite Consciousness, transmitted and adapted to this particular enclave.

Finally, we said that Ajna is sometimes represented by two wings. Two thoughts:
-Of course, the wings of the Dove, the Holy Spirit anointing the Christ. The being is ready for the anointment by the Holy Spirit and the Christ Consciousness. Also, the wings of the Spirit support him.

-With wings, one can fly, beyond the physical world, through multiple dimensions. The consciousness of the initiate is refined enough to give him access to parallel worlds. He can also travel in his light body, in awareness.

In conclusion, we will say that the sixth chakra opens the door to your Divine nature. It is the last one, still rooted on the body, to use your words, since the seventh is located above your physical self. Ajna is then the last link between Heaven and Earth. When he receives the Christ and the Holy Spirit, the being is open to the Divine State. His love, his intuition, his wisdom, clairvoyance, the mastery of polarities, all these lessons have been learned and understood. The Being is ready to receive the blessings of the coming back to the Whole, to the wombs of God and of the Mother, to the heart of the Universal Consciousness.

MERGING WITH THE GODSELF

It is easy to understand the pending relationship between the 6th center and the second. Ajna is the place of the merging. Merging is not only the fusion of the energies but also the marriage of the personality with the Godself. In the 5th the disciple already brought and developed his ability to create. But he was not anointed by the Holy Spirit, which means that he still had a tendency to will to create.

Through Ajna, creation and manifestation are just a state, the art of being opposed to personal will extended externally.

The relationship with God, the ease of the path, when one IS, allows the Holy Spirit to set in motion or activate whatever is necessary with his own divine energy and frequency, the frequencies of Love and Allowance. The initiate surrendered completely-"O my Father, Not as I will, but as Thou wilt" (Math. 26, 39). He is One with God, an instrument for the manifestation of God's perfection, through the Holy Spirit.

The disciple is asked to demonstrate trust and faith, instead of using his human wisdom or imagination in the process of creation. He might generate obstruction while thinking about what and how he is supposed to manifest. Dear Ones, I am using the verb to think, which means that the thought process is still implied and unfortunately the disciple does not free the way for Spirit to do the work. Nothing in this universe enters into existence unless someone, a being, would send out a thought, a preconceived idea of what they see or will. The idea, as soon as it is projected to the world immediately IS, but will not take form, unless and until, you detach yourself from it.

You understand, Beloved, that 'to do the work' is still a human way to design things. God does not do or work per se, He IS and emanates out of the womb and heart of His Being. The lesson is now to find the right balance between being and doing.

The sixth center is the fusion of everything that has been experienced within the other centers, in a river of understanding and surrender. The unobstructed stream created by the disciple is allowing his essence to merge with the formidable river of God's thought and Love.

There is nothing more beautiful than complete trust, trust in the beauty, trust in the completeness, trust in the achievement, which is the full circle after the meeting with the Inner God. There is nothing more beautiful than an initiate rejoicing every morning at the simple idea to be alive, admiring the splendor of creation and surrendering to God's flow. The being is no more into asking for himself, what he is supposed to produce, as you say in your human factories, he is just aligning himself with his blueprint, and then with the current, the electricity that is going to ignite the fire, to release the energy of manifestation.

I understand, Beloved Ones, that the state of BEING is not effortlessly stabilized on your plane. Humankind is still locked into the old programming. You still have the tendency to launch your command to any complying Veda and recreate your own old world, in maya. Instead, if you surrender to God and the Holy Spirit in humble, trusting collaboration, you will have the great joy and privilege to enter the perfection of the universe where love is the flow and the initiator, the match and the fire, the energy and the beginning, alpha and omega.

When one is ready for this level of surrendering, which is to stop thinking, to abandon the idea that you know what to do or what is good, or even your dreams, then you enter the core of the already existing perfect realm, the kingdom of universal creation.

When one is accepting that more exquisite dreams, passionate findings and innovations will occur as soon as he stop willing and thinking his own way, then, the miracle of God's presence will happen.

The blossoming of the I AM Divine Presence or DIVINE ESSENCE is the coming together of one's structure, heart/mind with the core, the heart/mind of God, where no separation exists, just deep and complete ONENESS with the Creator of Creators, the Infinite heart/mind of unfathomable majesty.

Be immensely blessed, Beloved Readers, in full Oneness and surrender. Experience the sweetness of God.

CHAKRA #7—SAHASRARA

I AM THAT I AM

I AM God, I AM the Presence, I AM God and Buddha.

The seventh center is the blossoming of the self in the Divine Consciousness. In order for Sahasrara to function entirely, all the other centers have to be built and clarified.

We will only briefly speak about the seventh chakra at this time as the entire second part of this book is about the multiple aspects of the blossoming of SAHASRARA.

As soon as I started to write this page a dove began to coo and warble a divine melody on the window. Close your eyes and ask, from the bottom of your heart, without any condition, for the Presence of God. In silence, feel the vastness of the World, the brightness of the Light, the sweetness of the Mother, the power of the Whole, the compassion of the Lords, Angels, Archangels, the laughter of the children and fairies. Listen to the indescribable music of the spheres. When all these blessings, all these emotions are pouring into your heart, into your cells, when you are One with all this beauty and dance, rocked in the arms of no time, then, you have a glimpse, you start com-prehending the energy of the seventh center.

The seventh center is a One Thousand-fold Lotus pointed down, on the top of your physical body, with the stem of the flower reaching out to Heaven. The stem is an antenna, a bridge between Heaven and Earth. When this connection is established you are continuously nurtured by the flow of God's Consciousness, the blessings of God's Love. You are aware of being a part of Him, Being Him, and stand, in the perpetual bliss inherent to your own Divinity.

SEVENTH CHAKRA AND EGOIC LOTUS

As an extension of the principle, "As above, so below" or a consequence of our belonging to a Whole, any action, any thought in any dimension affects the Whole. We are thus simultaneously working and expanding all of the levels of the self. The building of the chakras is a natural consequence of the interaction of the body and the soul. Simultaneously taking place is the construction, on the monadic plane of another piece of our magnificent multi-fold structure, the Lotus Egoic. The Lotus is a reflection of everything that the being is, that he has already integrated. It is called the "Center of the Heart of the Monad, correspondent to the heart center in the monadic manifestation." (Michel Coquet). It is the sum of everything, all the frequencies that one has already gathered, integrated through the threefold path of service, knowledge and love, as stated by the Tradition.

SERVICE, KNOWLEDGE and LOVE are the three principles implied in self-realization, the introduction of the Buddha's frequency in the individual structure.

KNOWLEDGE—AWARENESS

I have already spoken about knowledge in the previous chapter. I should add that a minimum of the culture of the spiritual and mystic Tradition is useful but not fundamental. Why? Do you need to read Sanskrit or Aramaic, to know the Kabbalah or the Bhagavad Gita to FEEL the Beauty and Love of the Creator?

So, what is this about? It is the intimate consciousness of the true nature of the vital force, thus of the Creator, developed and externalized in matter, through the various levels of the creation, vegetal, mineral, animal, human and spiritual. It is the intuition-we will later speak about cognition-of the multiple aspects of the Whole, the prehension of the omniscient, omnipresent, and eternal, unfathomable, indefinable nature of the One.

What is the profound nature of the vital force?

1.   The vital force, manifestation of the Infinite Consciousness, expresses itself freely, inexorably in the whole universe. It is the force breathed in by the heart/mind of God or expression of the intrinsic nature of God. It is omnipresent, eternal. The vital force inhabits and animates each parcel of the universe, One and Whole, undifferentiated. The form that it materializes as is not important. The gigantic body of a planet, a hurricane, any animated beings-which means in possession of a soul-the rocks, the plants are all a holographic expression of the vital force, a temporary condensation of energy.

2.   Specifications of the vital force:
-    Full surrender to the vital force is inevitable, it is the key to perfection manifested in any creature and in the life of the initiate.
-    The vital force is double in nature, only complete when merging the two opposites.
-    Moves and exists according to its own laws and trajectory.

Surrender to the divine presence is manifested by the acceptance of the divine will in your daily life and the surrender to the uninterrupted flow of the vital force.

KNOWING THROUGH THE HEART — THE PATH OF UNCONDITIONAL LOVE

Knowing through the heart, through feelings instead of the brain is the key to easy and absolute alignment with God. I am not saying that it is enough to have passed some of the initiations in this galaxy and to have opened the seven chakras to be technically and suddenly an ascended Master or to understand, with your limited brain the totality of the mysteries and the divine nature. Although all the species, human and non human, who decided to join each other on planet earth gained much from specific and exceptional conditions of growth and spiritual evolution, it is impossible, in a body, to apprehend the Infinite Consciousness. But, and there lies the secret, if you transfer your cognition center from the brain to the heart, then, you are no longer limited by the mathematical needs of the brain. You are in alignment, in symbiosis with the frequency that guides you further than intuition, that is to say the vibration of the emotions.

I will use a very simple example. As human beings, you have difficulties understanding the language of the Ascended Masters, and their answers to what seems so important to you, living in the third dimension. The language of the angels, their way of intervening or their rules of non-intervention feel sometimes strange to you. And above all, the agenda of the Sons of Spirit seems too slow for you. Although the shift has already started, you are impatient because you still live in time. And, time does not exist as soon as you ARE.

Please, Dear Ones, stop thinking in the third dimensional mode. All of your concepts, laws and principles are changing. Learn how to feel, emote. Instead of analyzing a situation, ask yourself how your body, your heart feels it.

When your are asked to do something, when you meet someone, listen to your feelings or immediate physical reactions. Are you happy, in peace, or are you operating against your heart feelings?

In the cycles of evolution of the race, the last important shift happened with the introduction of the MIND QUALITY. This was the introduction in the human structure of the capacity to analyze, discern, discuss and make a decision. Instead of existing like innocent babies, in the beatitude resulting in total trust and a state of non-question, the being, the soul had to experience life momentarily separated* from God's aura. This experience led to self-consciousness, expansion and ultimately to the return to the WHOLE, with the capacity to create.

Spirit descended into form, allows consciousness to discover and integrate the principle of duality:

1.   Life and any expression of life
-    Proceeds from the Whole

-    Expresses itself by extreme or opposite feelings generating dual or extreme situations: Love/hate, faith/fear, gratitude/jealousy, forgiveness/resentment...

-    Is the physical manifestation, in the third dimension, of two opposite and complementary forces, Yin/Yang, positive/negative, male/female, Light/shadow, Spirit and Matter.

-    Reproduces and balances itself when those two forces are merging. The marriage or fusion of the energies allows the stabilization in perfection and bliss, which emanate from the frequency of the MIDDLE PATH, the path out of duality, without extremes or polarities.
-    Returns to the Whole when reaching the DIVINE STATE, fused and United, in the peace of AWARENESS—as the Knower, detached from the need to understand, to question, to reproduce, to act.

2.   There is no superior or inferior principle. The two qualities, Light and Shadow, are two expressions of the One Infinite Consciousness and are completing each other.

3. Any voluntary stoppage in the extremes, or choice to live a polarity with excess is a source of difficulty, sorrow and leads to a plethora of one quality of energy, instead of a balance of both. This lack of equilibrium, of harmony is the cause of all the diseases and especially of depression, which is a plague in our modern society.

The integration of the faculty of reasoning and/of the mind was appropriate in the meeting of the human being with MATTER and with the SHADOW. The cycle that is now ending for humankind was the era of the introduction into the consciousness of the concept of duality. It is now time to let go of duality.

[Beloved, while putting these in the form of notes for editing, I have to emphasize the quasi-impossibility of using terms that are accurate as soon as one expands his consciousness beyond the third dimension. Although I use words like "separation", "exterior", "lower", "superior", "far", none of these terms are exact, when one is aware of Wholeness, Oneness.]

The cycles through which the human being is evolving are an extension and a picture of the cycles through which the Infinite Consciousness Itself is moving, breathing. The universes are the externalization of the divine breath, each inhale-exhale manifesting two aspects of the Whole.

We already spoke in I AM THAT I AM of the significance of the word "knowledge", using the French translation: "The goal of the creature is not only to refine his consciousness, but also to reach Consciousness by the Co-Knowledge, the revelation of his true nature. In French, knowledge is Connaissance, a word that we can divide into Co-Naissance—Naissance is birth. Then, Co-Naissance literally means Co-Birth, a new birth induced through awareness."

Let us add that the being who reaches the divine, to the point that he feels himself not only a part of the Whole but the All in One has access to the frequency of the Co-creation. He is no longer isolated. He is bathing in the re-discovery of the self, as a god. He is not at the mercy of the old systems that enslaved him. He is the ecstatic beneficiary of the totality of the gifts offered to the children of the Universe.

KNOWLEDGE AND COGNITION— MIND AND HEART

While journeying from the mind vibration to the heart vibration, the being brings forth the lotus or center of the monadic consciousness.

The first row of petals appears as a result of knowledge, the second row of petals from the integration of love as the essence of the Self. When one goes beyond the stage of learning through books, the accumulation of logical facts and proofs, he will naturally reach intuitive knowledge, based on self-confidence and trust in divine guidance.

This state of consciousness, connecting knowledge with love is not established in a linear way, in time. Knowledge creates love and love engenders a flow of intuitive understanding and knowing. It is in fact the quality, the essence, the manner of dealing with situations that is evolving in conjunction with the acquisition of knowledge and the refinement of the individual and of his soul.

SILENCE AND RETREAT

In order to enjoy a more intimate relationship with the divine presence, the disciple will develop the habit of staying in silence and retreat.

When a being is not refined he needs constant distraction and amusement for his senses. Because he is not in communication, in harmony with his intimate nature, his soul, he lives outside of himself. The sensations produced by others, the noise, the movement or agitation are the triggers he needs to activate his nervous system. His existence is still similar to the expression of life as it was instituted in Lemuria. As this time, the reptilians were so close to the earth energy that a group of their representatives were crawling on the ground. Their brain was barely developed their bodies less sophisticated than the structure that we know today. The race was undergoing the maturation of the parasympathetic nervous system. In other words, the beings living on the planet developed reflex reactions to specific situations in order to adjust to living on this planet. Starting in Atlantis, the race began to enjoy sensations; the race began to build the emotional body. The emotional body exists as a response to external sensations; in fact it is a social envelope. The quality of the emotions that one accepts and cultivates-thoughts and capacity to master drama or peace—defines (determines) the kind of emotional body that will be constructed. For instance, a depression can originate with the decision to concentrate on only one thought or challenge, and then to be so centered on this situation alone, that no detachment is possible. A cocoon of energy is created, reflecting the being's own enslavement. This cocoon will separate the person from the exterior world. He/She does not see, hear, enjoy any communication with others. A depressed person actually has a tendency to literally retreat in dark rooms.

When an individual is humanly sane, he will look for pleasure. Of course, a disciple will control any tendency to jump to the extremes: constant sexual stimulation, alcohol and drugs, incapability to live without a crowd around him, loud music, all of these leading to an inability to be and think by himself.

The being who searches God's Presence sits alone every day to pray and meditate. First as discipline, then as pleasure, he enjoys calm and silence. In stillness, he finally hears the voice of the soul and of the Infinite Consciousness.

The more the individual progresses in the refinement of consciousness and of his spiritual structure, the more he will look for periods of retreat. Far from the others, from the noise and agitation, he perceives the subtleties of the invisible planes. He opens up to the presence of higher beings and improves his intuition, clairvoyance, clairaudience, although none of these are indispensable.

Also, when one retires at least once a day, he clears his etherical body from all interactions, all emotions tiredness. Finally, it is a good habit to retreat for a seven-day period, once a year, if possible in nature. The disciple will re-adjust himself with the Mother, the earth, the physical elements, and will meet with his soul.

****

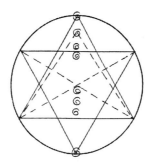

SIX-POINTED STAR

SACRED GEOMETRY

If we shift from a philosophical context to a scientific and mathematical one, God would probably be easier to comprehend. At the end of this century, you are blessed with new information, allowing science to explain and confirm the old Tradition that at one time was classified as Magic. Indubitably, the elders had an intuitive understanding of the cosmos and of its laws, but rarely did people have access to the information that is available to the public now.

You can imagine the Creator as an extraordinary force, gifted with feelings, love, projecting Himself in the infinite space, through his mind. He exteriorizes/externalizes waves that are translated into mathematical formulas, then into genetic codes and then into creatures.

The codes imprinted in the creation are transmitted through geometrical patterns, commonly called sacred geometry. Creation evolves and becomes sophisticated through the integration within itself of simple but precise geometrical forms, such as the square, the triangle, the circle, the pentagram, and the hexagram. In three dimensions, these shapes are the cube, the pyramid, the tetrahedron, the sphere, the star tetrahedron, etc. These geometrical patterns are imprinted in the cells, in the DNA. They are visible by the clairvoyant, in people's structure and on the aura.

The GEOMETRICAL CODES imprinted in all of creation, physical or subtle are God's imprint. They ARE:

- The PATTERNS on which matter, physical or subtle, builds itself. Atoms, crystals, plants and the human body all contain, immutably, the same geometrical symbols in their structure.

- The KEYS speaking to our subconscious and unconscious. Elders, advanced souls knew about the existence of sacred geometry. This explains why the simplest forms, such as the cube, the sphere, the six pointed star, the flower of life were used in the mystery schools, the churches or sacred sites, to call back or wake up the students' consciousness.

- TOOLS to evolve faster
  You can utilize sacred geometry in a very simple and very efficient way. If you believe that everything is energy, that you are only a holographic image, you understand that you can influence, modify a hologram, with your thoughts.

  For instance, if you want to introduce into your DNA the pyramidal shape, you can spend your vacations in the great pyramid or build one in copper and meditate in it. The shape of the building will broadcast its energy-message to you. But nothing is more effective than the sincere wish and intent, combined with visualization. In fact, you visualize on you, in you and around you the geometrical forms that you wish to imprint and reflect in your structures, as YOURSELF.

When one knows about the circulation and distribution of the energies in the universe and in the body, it is even easier to mimic and align yourself, put yourself in harmony with the laws of creation of the cosmos, by the action of repeating these laws with your mind. For instance: three lines of forces/energy must link the pituitary gland, the pineal gland and the Alta Major. Then, why not visualize these connections of energy to amplify and quicken the phenomenon? (See I AM THAT I AM, Section II, chapter one and Section IV, chapter three). In this book we will present the most simple but essential geometrical shapes, for the present time. However, other geometrical codes do exist, such as the flower of life, that you might want to use, according to your achievement and needs.

We will add, that, according to our experience, toning or the use of sounds is one of the quickest techniques to create a shift, a change. Sounds clear the energies, immediately alter the state of consciousness, break the blocks and create the necessary geometrical patterns, in the moment, for your growth.

The six-pointed star, as most of ancient symbols is to be read and interpreted from several points of view, several dimensions. The hexagram is composed of two equilateral triangles. The equilateral triangle represents the harmonious, perfectly balanced inter-action of three forces, which attract each other and complete each other.
The base of the triangle is the space from where the experience is happening, or sensed. The apex is the focus, the goal, the place that the consciousness is exploring or in the process of reaching.

TRIANGLE POINTED UP

It is a representation of MATTER. The being experiences incarnation, physicality. He is incarnated in a body and endures the illusion generated by the loss of Self, the Separation, the fall into the physical dimension.

When a soul leaves the divine womb for the great crusade, it has to build a material counterpart, a reflection and stabilize it. This is the phase of integration of the square and the cube. The soul is incorporating the physical elements of the universe and densifying itself to the point of motionlessness, as a rock.

On the plane of manifestation, two principles inter-act, oppose and then unite with each other in order to create: Yin/Yang, Shadow/Light, Female/male, negative/positive. Each of these principles or qualities is associated with specific states of consciousness, related to antagonistic feelings.

In the third dimension, matter, life expresses itself most often through feelings that we will call, for better denomination, negative, unbalanced, violent, and destructive. In the spiritual dimensions, the vital force manifests itself in a constructive, positive way, through unconditional love, beauty, peace, joy, etc.

The physical world is a reflection, a hologram projected by/on our consciousness, a momentary and conditional 'densification' of the thoughts that you broadcast, merged with those of the people that you have invited into your conscious life/universe. In this domain, you discover and then learn to evolve through laws and opposite principles. These principles are a manifestation or a representation of the extreme vibrations existing in the universe, of the scale of states, feelings emanating from the two basic forces that are completing, marrying each other in matter.

While in incarnation, the being is looking upward, his eyes and heart looking toward Spirit, Heaven, God. He intuitively or sometimes in confusion remembers his origin and works at returning home, in the bosom of the Creator God. He is on the path to evolution, ascension.

The triangle pointed up is often used to represent the Monad. It is then the positive aspect of the triangle pointed up, the pure expression of Spirit descended AND incarnated.

TRIANGLE POINTED DOWN

When God started to create, outside of Himself, He inaugurated the cycles of expansion, contraction or descension, ascension. Spirit looking for physical extension, expression, had to descend towards the material planes. The involution or densification process is the triangle pointed down.

As ascension means enlightenment or increase of the amount of Light within the structure of a being, descension is the progressive invasion of the self by the shadow, or voluntary abandon of the being to the experience of darkness.

Then, it is easy to understand that the negative aspect of this triangle would be an excess of materialization, or an excessive attraction to the shadow, or a complete loss of the self which is in fact amnesia of the Divine. In this case, the triangle pointed down is an image of the creature in pain, lost in matter, and absorbed in hurtful experiences.

In our discourse about manifestation, this triangle is a powerful picture of Heaven descending on Earth. The Spiritual Beings, the Ascended Masters, the Angels and Archangels are advancing, progressing towards matter, towards Mother Earth, towards you.

CHRIST CONSCIOUSNESS

Christ consciousness is the center. No matter what name or term that you use, it is the state of being (Etat d'Etre), the vibration of the being positioned, anchored in the heart center, the end of one's floundering between the extremes, white and black, sorrow, fear. Christ Consciousness is the end of Duality. It is to know and to be the equilibrium, in serenity. A "Christ" is also aware of his position/action into the Whole, as One. He has an inner knowing, consciousness, of the meaning of what humans call a holographic image, where the core is the whole and the whole is core. You, we, I all participate, are, in God's breath, as his own breath, as Him, inter-connectedly. Each and every breath of a creature, Beloved Brothers and Sisters, or thought creates a universe.

A Christed being embodies the six-pointed star. He worked and completed the structure of 2 X 3 chakras, the two triangles and fused them in his heart. It is the completion of a cycle. The being has the intimate awareness, consciousness of matter and spirit, of the macrocosm and microcosm. He came back to himself, complete. The dot in the center of the circle.

****

I AM Michael and my energy is coiled into your heart, beats through your heart. And yet, I am not fully residing in the physical world. I AM Michael and you are Michael, We are One, the same being, living and breathing at the same beat, nurtured by the same life force or same holy blood, and yet, we are appearing as two interconnected beings, projected in two separate dimensions.

What does this mean? When you call upon me and feel more of my Divine Presence in your human/god heart, you do feel a stream of love penetrating and warming up your physical organ. And yet you know and you feel, every day a little more, as Archangel Michael. The secret is the heart.

When both triangles have been duly completed, the Being is ready for the spiritual marriage. In his heart, already illuminated and turned upward-see I Am THAT-a seed is blossoming; the Monad is anchoring itself.

You are blessed, Beloved One, because at this period in time, you are guided, infused by two influxes, one sent by the Presence and the other by the Christ. These two forces penetrate the heart and root themselves in it.

The heart chakra, in fact, plays two roles. In the first part of the disciple's life, up to the sixth initiation, the heart contains the germ of the Soul and allows communication with others and with God through feelings, emotions. Almost confusedly, humankind started to speak about love, unconditional openness to others as the magical way. Man, coming out of thousands of years of emotional imprisonment, habits and narrow minded traditions thought that he was expressing divine love, through and only through his body. In fact, Beloved, it was a sound reflex, because the human being, divinely inspired was anchoring himself in matter and allowed the third dimension to be the revealer of God's Spirit, of the spiritual force manifesting itself on earth. Then, in the second step, the disciples believed that it was time to consecrate (make sacred) their impulse/needs for physical bondage by adding an emotional and then a spiritual aspect to it.

With the Christ, another relationship, let us say, without judgement, a little more refined, is established between Human being, soul and Monad. It is the fusion of three worlds. A human being recognizes himself in God. He loves and marries his own godself. Doing so, he opens a channel of energy. The divine flow, the Presence circulates freely in the multi and inter-dimensional vehicle of the being. The heart chakra is the center in the physical part of this immense structure. But it is only an atom in the whole edifice, or more exactly the reflection on the physical plane of the spiritual heart whose energy or code is imprinted in all physical atoms. It is the mystery of the infinitely great reproduced in the infinitely small.

The Christ, God's direct and unique son, is the fastest link to the Creator. He showed the path to humankind, a path that you are taking: A divine being concludes an agreement with one or several humans, that is to say with the tri-dimensional world: announcement to Mary and contract with the human Jesus. Jesus had been prepared by studying the Tradition, with the Essenes and his practice to connect himself with God.

When the time had come, Jesus fused/merged himself with the Divine, in this case the Christ. He remembered, became Jesus Christ. He then demonstrated publicly what it means to embody the Father, the magic of love combined with power and detachment. Not only did he reveal extraordinary powers, but also he touched the crowds with his presence and love alone.

Jesus Christ planted a seed in the aura of the planet, so that a great number of incarnated souls, lost in matter, would remember their origin and open themselves enough to make the fusion possible. These beings are the BODY OF THE CHRIST on earth, the body birthing the Christ consciousness and the redemption of the race.

The initiates who accomplished the triple task of knowing, serving and loving (three ranges of petals of the lotus, see I AM, chapter One) have been reproducing this miracle. The life of the Monad can bloom in their heart. These initiates are also the BODY of the DIVINE PRESENCE or BODY of I AM on the planet. They are the core around which the Creator can anchor Himself to envelope, enshroud and divinize, again, all the creation.

If you are open, telepathically receptive, you will have more contacts with the beings or energies that are the grid of your system. Each of you will hear the piece for which you are encoded. Each piece of the puzzle will be activated, when the time is right. It is not necessary to hurry, to try becoming a channel or a master. All of you Beloved ARE MASTERS, and all of you are channels, because we are ONE. BEING is the key. We repeat, "Being" is to stay centered, in love, in God's heart.

Below are the most important words, now, in the terrestrial journey, that you can use, every morning, to anchor your day.

I AM . . . . , I AM GOD
One in the heart of God
One with the heart beat of the Universe
One with the heart/mind of God
I AM in harmony with God, with One.

Be my life, now manifested on the physical plane
A pure reflection, manifestation on the third dimension
Of love, beauty, joy, harmony, peace
Health, abundance, reflection of God the Creator.

Be this day, in the now and in eternity
A pure manifestation, in the third dimension,
Of my Divineness

I AM MICHAEL
I AM THAT I AM
SO BE IT. NOW

******

The heart is more than a symbol; it is the organ marking your rhythm, your pulse, your resonance. If this organ is ready to receive, continuously, the Presence, it will automatically beat in harmony with the Divine Creator.

This is the reason why it is important to cleanse your emotional miasms. We are not, Beloved Ones, minimizing your human love, human painful experiences; we are just guiding you through their transmutation in order for you to become transparent. If one keeps the pain, he is attached to his pain. God is attached neither to the pain nor to the happiness, because for Him, these distinctions do not exist, as they seem to in the third dimension. The feelings or re-actions to pain or joy only persist and keep you separated from peace, serenity and from the state of BEING.

In the heart is a thread that links us mechanically, to the HEART OF THE SUN, the heart of the system your belong to NOW.

PRINCIPLES SYMBOLIZED/ENCODED BY THE HEXAGRAM

As above, so below.
Marriage of Heaven and Earth
Heaven on Earth
Fusion of Matter and Spirit
Inter-dimensional fusion

SECTION II

PRINCIPLES OF
MANIFESTATION

PRINCIPLE #1 — BE AND SURRENDER

"NOT MY WILL, FATHER, BUT THINE BE DONE"

A moment comes, during the pilgrim's life, when through comprehension or lassitude, the walker decides to put down his stick and stop. I will again disclose my own story to illustrate this chapter.

****

When I entered the galaxy with the Sanat Kumara, it was by choice. I had always been a part of the Lodge of the Light. But, truly, the journey on planet Earth had been, hum, interesting, full of excitement as American people would say-sorry Beloved Readers; I am still amused by this word. I created for myself many spicy challenges, many rides, and sometimes chaos.

There was this extraordinary council on planet Sirius. Human beings did not evolve fast enough. The normal tactic of the two lodges-the White One and the Black One-is to walk graciously on the chessboard, exchange some stakes and perform pirouettes. It is essential, in order for the universes to keep their inexorable moves, that the light and the shadow always stay balanced. But the consciousness of human beings was not being touched, not to the point of being able to transmute the Yin and the Yang and of reaching the divine frequency, the marriage.

This is why, in the crystal palace where they were meeting, an unusual uproar started. Everyone was expressing his opinion. Do we have the right to intervene directly? Were we going to implant a new grid of command, in order to precipitate the marriage of the energies? The brothers of the shadow and the brothers of the light have always respected each other, each group having an impact on the march of the world and the earthly horde. But it is true that the extremes induce complicated or even dishonorable situations, considered from a human point of view. In the case of the human family, the desire to experience matter increased century after century, guided by the old Saturn, Master of Time and density. The Taurus era was at the door, with the god Molock...

The grand council finally made a decision. Some of the members of the White Lodge had even forgotten their secret encoding. They had forgotten who they were, what their mission was, on the earth and with the Hierarchy. Since Egypt, they were the guardians of the Tradition and keepers of the Light. But, little by little, through too many and too dense incarnations, they had become like the others, human. They did not remember the sacred chants, they lost the keys. Just like the others, they were eager for power and sex. Of course, the sacred rites had been introduced. In order to honor the Serpent, to make the humans, now as dense as rocks, vibrate again, they had decided to use the lower life energy, sex, desire, pleasure.

This had been a difficult choice, the Council was divided. Were we going, in order to remember the divine path, the joy of Unity, the great marriage, to use sexual pleasure? What was the risk? For some, whose hearts were still connected with the heart of the Sun and the heart of God, the trick immediately worked. They mastered their power and their life force, while feeling the awakening of the Serpent, at the base of their spine. However, very few were successful in achieving the sacred merging. The priestesses were beautiful. A lot of members, whether under male or female physical masks, succumbed. Not that sex and pleasure is reprehensible, but the priest and the wise man are supposed to remember the hidden secrets behind it. They were supposed to honor the Serpent, instead of the vase carrying it, instead of the dances and the sensations.

A lot of moons went by over the Nile, the Euphrates, and the brothers of the Light were lost. The amnesic ones scattered throughout the world. Unfortunately a group was tempted by the powerful rites of their twin brothers, the guardians of the Shadow. The shadow grew in power in the sacred mystery schools.

In the Grand Council, the Elders were watching the situation. It was time to intervene. The restoration of the memories of the Brothers and of the human beings might take millions of years. The Tradition had been twisted, the feminine lineage almost destroyed.

The Elders knew that is was the wisest solution, the closest to the truth. They will have to reproduce the law of the marriage in the second and third dimension. Nothing in this universe is complete without the fusion of the energies, of the extremes. Human beings had the habit of taking refuge in the illusion, duplicating it through shows, rituals, in which they would call for the ones they were mistaking for gods. As soon as a Stranger would appear on Earth in a ship or wearing clothing of Light, humans would become enthralled.

The council decided then to use the temples, the sacred schools, the priests, and the rituals. The fusion of the energies, the marriage of the Light and the Shadow will be part of the sacred ceremonies. The shock generated on the genetic codes, the interference with the soul, will be so severe, that the initiate, hurt and in pain, would have to return to the light in order to re-center himself. The initiate will come back in full awareness, complete, conscious. Never more, will he be lost, because his memories would have been imprinted by the experience. The dark initiation was born.

Of course, the Brothers of the Light will be at the center of the experience. They had, in their blood and in their magnetic structure the purest codes, the original ones. Although some of them had already been altered by genetic manipulations, the Elders will find a way to overcome this handicap. In fact, the challenge was interesting.

All of this, I, Nora-Michael, Brother of the Light, remembered. The dive into matter had shocked me, of course, but not as much as the agreement that I had made, in service to the Lodge. I had already remembered, but accepted to come back in a female body, a young girl. I will give myself as a sacrifice to the Forces of the Shadow and will open a doorway, communicate with a great number of dark lodges. I will end several lineages of shadow workers, helping them to transmute their energies.

This last lifetime on earth had been such a trip. I was called, to visit and clear all kinds of groups, spiritual schools, some of them so secret, that only my faculty to navigate inter-dimensionally and to read the Akashic records was useful. A friend once described the apparatus that was set around me to accomplish this work. "Nora-Michael was standing in the center of a sphere of light and fire, of which the edges were cobalt blue and golden. Around her, were agglutinated, like bees on honey, all the thought forms, The entities seeking for transmutation or trying to hoard some of her powerful energy. Some dark life forms, too dense to even be conscious of the process, were just attracted and were being nurtured with Light."

I knew that this part of my work had come to an end. In 1996 and 1997, I attended several inter-dimensional councils related to the end of the Pisces era. Below a narration of these events, already published in a newsletter:

Message of the Great White Brotherhood

To our Beloved Human Brothers and Sisters:

A long time ago, hand in hand with the Planetary Hierarchy and the Sanat Kumara, we initiated the Great White Brotherhood in order to carry the Light to this planet and to ensure that, whatever the challenges, together, we and you would remain on the path of Love, Light-Consciousness and Freedom. Some of us made the commitment to incarnate in human bodies and to struggle along with you. Why?

- To deliver and to share with mankind the Energy of the Hierarchy, to be living imprints of this frequency among you, and to travel to specific areas as the need arises.
- To imprint the Light frequency through genetics.
- To be physically present within some of your groups and organizations in order to guide, straighten situations, and balance the Energies each time the Shadow should become too powerful.
- To experience the human path and thus efficiently help you.

Our name and functions have been misunderstood and misused a number of times all throughout history. It is true that some of our members, by necessity or overwhelmed by physicality, even participated in what you refer to as the Shadow. The path of Conscious Light reveals great mysteries and the balancing of the energies is still to be understood fully by you, Beloved.

All over the planet, a great awakening is taking place and we are very sensitive to your progress. However, and this is why we decided to speak up, we would like to prevent some situations from reoccurring. We are so close to seeing the Essence of Love established on Planet Earth! Our Lord, the Sanat Kumara is directing his boundless Love Energy through the heart of Christ and experiencing joy when you respond, and accept your true responsibilities on the path of Initiation.

Changes have been occurring in an accelerated mode since **May 1996**. Decisions were made during the Wesak festival in order to assist the Sanat Kumara in his work as the carrier of your planet. A plan was set up and applied at the time of the Equinox by the wondrous beings that are embodying the planets involved in your spiritual system. Let us describe what happened in human words and images:

The active members of the Great White Brotherhood are gathered in the room of "The Twelve".

Standing up in a powerful, meditative circle, we strike up together the equinox chant. Rapidly the sounds are generating a dome of energy above us, whose apex is pointed toward the Galaxy.

Sanat Kumara appears, by Himself. From the center of his total being, from four main rays, emerges a form, the imprint of a majestic and powerful face, a reflection of his personality. The Sanat Kumara blesses the room and his energy merges with the dome-sum of the vibrations of the Great White Brotherhood members.

The six other Kumaras, three on each side, now surround Sanat Kumara. The seven merge together as a unique body.

At this point, the 7 brothers position themselves as a line in order to welcome the 7 wives, the Pleiades. The marriage takes place according to a linear and crossed pattern. A complete inter-relation of the energies—male/female/7 frequencies—is renewed for the month and year to come.

Then the intergalactic Princes and Lords of neighboring planets arrive from all the directions and introduce themselves to participate in the ongoing ceremony. A magnificent ballet is now occurring wrapped in the celestial colors and lights of the space and bathed in a subtle music. According to the systemic scheme, the vibrations of the terrestrial and solar Hierarchies are building and organizing. In a sublime dance/meditation, the Kumaras and the Pleiades harmonize themselves with their galactic companions.

Each planetary energy is experimented individually and separately by the attendants, then implanted in our systems. We are infused by the blended energy of the galaxy, so that its pattern, its frequency, deeply imprinted in the Lodge may be redistributed.

Finally, the Kumaras stand by themselves, in the center of the ceremony. They are now merging in order to form a unique ray, harmonized on the cardiac chakra. This Christic ray enters each member through his own cardiac center. Then, the ray successively touches the sole of our feet, the palms, the throat, and the forehead. We are all vibrating in unison, nurturing ourselves with this conjugated power. Next, the ray clarifies our main chakras, which begin to gleam and open themselves even more, as magnificent corollas. A serpentine, fire like energy, coils itself, merges with our glorious bodies.

The Kumaras leave, the brothers bend over, on their knees, and give thanks for the privilege and joy of participating in the work of the Hierarchy. The members of the Great White Lodge then position themselves to form an intricate precise pattern, based on multiple of 12. This model will allow the attendants to scatter all over the planet and to broadcast the vibratory flux generated during the ceremony." (Excerpted from I Am That I Am, Alta Major).

A new phase occurred for the *full moon of January*. We were very happy to notice the presence of a great number within the human plane. Because of your increased level of awareness, your ability to feel, understand astrology, and the wonderful work done by channels, the light workers were ready and supported the Hierarchy through their thoughts and meditation.

The alignment of planets that you were all awaiting, was a gathering of beings, willing to open a passage and diffuse a specific energy, which will create a bridge that your Lord, Sanat Kumara, will use in order to be able to raise his/your vibrations in order to be fully prepared for the Aquarius era. This energy, blue in color, was sent from your Universal Sun, to cleanse planet Earth.

Then the Lords of the planets present at the meeting turned their attention to the body of the Sanat Kumara. A clearing was conducted on his lungs, in order to remedy the pollution problem. In this regard, the opening of the magnetic "ring pass not"* also permitted the arrival in your atmosphere of a new gas. This will complete the necessary cleansing of the planet's respiratory system.

Finally the Masters turned their attention to the Sanat Kumara's feet and removed an old energy from them, a vibration, which was holding him in the Pisces frequency. This movement makes the dimensional shift in mankind and mother Earth easier to complete by the Sanat Kumara and he will thus be fully prepared for the beginning of the Aquarius Age.

This movement in the planets and the voluntary opening of your ring pass not are facilitating the arrival of the comet Hale-Bopp and her companion. These bodies are bringing to planet Earth the Sacred 6 pointed star energy field. The opening in the aura of planet earth as well as the arrival of the 6 pointed star generate powerful consequences for your immediate future and life on the planet.

-   The Light will no longer arrive to you in a veiled way.
    Human structures, physical and spiritual will thus transmute easily and more naturally. Your glands, your cells, your atomic anatomy will be affected, allowing your transformation.

-   The star will act as a filter to protect your planet from many disruptive energies and entities.

-   Manifestation is made easier on the physical plane. This is to be understood at two different levels:
•   Those of you who have been striving to achieve their spiritual goals will feel more empowered and see their creation manifested in their life.
•   The Sanat Kumara will be able to broadcast and manifest his intent, love, and vibration throughout the planet. In clear, this means an improvement in the conditions of life on Earth, even if the labor is sometimes difficult. For instance, as already channeled, volcanic activities and earthquakes may be part of

the growing process, especially in areas that you consider as safe and stable. The imprint and the grounding of the Masters' energy on different regions of the earth will be cleared, renewed and thus telluric activities will occur.

- The Great White Brotherhood will soon emerge and change its way of action. For the first time since its appearance within your system, its role and members are to be more apparent and known to the public, in order to directly assist individuals, groups, governments.

- Changes took place in the Hierarchy. Several High Masters left to pursue their work in other systems and their positions were filled by new figures, trained for centuries and waiting in Tibet.

- Growing pains are to be felt within the main organized churches and mystery schools.

Great steps are still to be taken in the next few weeks, and until the full moon of March, such as the atonement/balancing of the dual frequencies, through the heart-mid February. This will harmonize the presence of what you call the Shadow and allow the true Power of Spiritual Love to be anchored within mankind.

EQUINOX, MARCH 20TH, 1997.

The energies of the planet as well as the energy of the Sanat Kumara, Lord of the Planet, have been deeply renewed during the past several weeks. Literally surrounded and supported by the Lords of the neighboring planets, the Sanat Kumara, in a state of intense meditation, semi-cataleptic, was immersed in a tremendous vortex of energy for several weeks. We know that, for the full moon of January, the planets were positioned to form a perfect star of David-as seen on a two dimensional picture. During this Ceremony, the Sanat Kumara was cleared from the remaining frequencies of the Pisces and prepared for the Aquarius Era. Since then, He has been gathering all his strength, supported by the blessings and vibrational impact of his heavenly companions. Throughout the day of the Equinox, several geometrical patterns were imprinted/anchored on the etherical body of the planet, through the channels of the Planetary Hierarchy and the White Lodge.

One of those patterns was the 6-pointed star. This symbol can be extended as a 3 or 4 dimensional figure. It is the pattern of the merging of Matter and Spirit, the at-one-ment of the Earth with the Spiritual planes. This pattern was broadcast all day and will stay focused towards earth as long as Mankind needs this frequency.

However in order to help the planet and her children to raise its vibration, the Hierarchy projected and imprinted/encoded our atmosphere and the members of the Lodge with the holograms of:

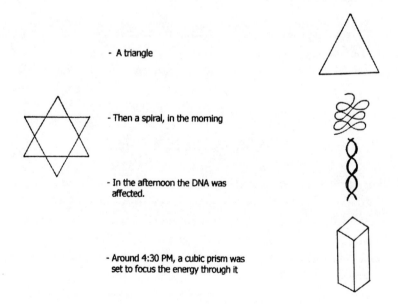

- A triangle

- Then a spiral, in the morning

- In the afternoon the DNA was affected.

- Around 4:30 PM, a cubic prism was set to focus the energy through it

Then the Pleiades and the Kumaras placed themselves in two semi-circles, facing each other, the Sun being North. The cosmic dance, involving the Pleiades and the Kumaras implied a merging of the Male and Female energies, following up of the major ceremony, which took place in June 1996. For 1997, the scheme of the Cosmic Hierarchy aims to assimilate the already merged vibration to the solar frequency, or divine/monadic one.

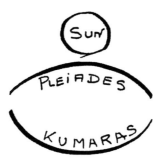

One can see slowly a new picture appearing in the cosmos, the Egyptian Eye. This symbol represents the integration of the spiritual Sun, in the bosom of the combined male/positive and female/negative vibrations. This way, the complete, androgynous frequency is generated; then following each other, the frequencies of the Serpent, the Christ sacrificed-merging into matter, the Christ glorified-returning to Spirit, with awareness.

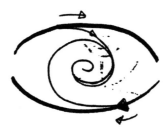

Bear in mind that Sanat Kumara holds and supports planet Earth in his meditation/breath. The planet is the physical body that he accepted to overshadow, through which he expresses Himself, in the same way we have a 3 dimensional body. For a long period of time, his physical body, if we may use such a language, has been polarized at the vibratory rate of the second chakra or sexual center, full expression of the duality and the instinct of intermingling/reproduction. What mankind needs to work on now is the merging of the male/ positive energy with the female/negative polarity. This fusion is to be located in the heart chakra. Doing so, you will reproduce what the Christ did. He merged the Energy of the Spirit, in a physical vehicle, and transcended his whole being out of matter, resurrecting Himself into a new dimension. He expresses thus the full meaning of Love which is the coming together of the polarities, the sharing, the surrendering to the point of merging, the marriage.

Similarly, mankind accepted the crusade in the physical body, has been experiencing the positive/male and negative/female (2nd and 3rd chakras) and is now ready for the merging in the heart (Glorified Christ frequency).

The Lords leading the ceremony are now activating and clarifying the 2nd and 3rd chakras of the planet, and thus of Mankind. The working out and expansion of the human energies through Hatha Yoga, with the physical body as the main tool is now coming to an end. The future will see the emergence of a new type of Yoga, more in harmony with a pure kundalinic energy. With the Yoga of the Chakras, implying the mind, humans will reach the level of the Glorified Christ, the merging.

Love signifies sharing, participation. Mankind still needs to heal itself.

ECLIPSE, MARCH 23RD.

The energy irradiating from the planetary alignment produces an immediate opening of the crown chakra. The result is so intense that the aura of the participants (Members of the White Lodge) is affected up to their arms and heart.

This energy is then re-transmitted by the members all over the planet (using specific points of the grid, vortices of the Great pyramid, Peru, China, Africa...). Then led by a high Master the members go to a spiritual temple, similar to a crystal temple. There, instructions are given on the way mankind is to be educated in the future months and years.

Mankind has to learn to develop the mind, mind energy as well as practicing telepathic imprint. This means to develop the intuition, the heart and the spiritual abilities, in order to communicate telepathically with other humans and with the invisible planes. It is a complete and aware communication, oneness with the body of the planet, the mind and the heart of the Sanat Kumara. Keep in mind the fact that the Aquarius is the Era of the group, the working together, which cannot really exist without an increased sensitivity and then a true participation in the life and evolution of the planet. The Lodge has to emphasize the necessity to direct the energies of the second chakra to the heart center. It is possible to physically assist human beings using magnetized water, imprinted with the energy of the six pointed stars and the whole Equinox Ceremony.

Also, the members are to teach, ask spiritual healers to free the feet of people, in the same way that the Sanat Kumara was cleared from the Pisces vibrations in order to reach the Aquarius frequency.

After being imprinted with the new cosmic energies, the Lodge is divided into three groups, based on the numbers 5, 5 and 2, which are escorted to a high mountain. The Sanat Kumara is there, present, ready to pass an initiation, supported by the planetary and solar Lords. His solar plexus is cleansed. Then he receives a ray from Mercury, which stimulates his head centers and mind.

Then the abdominal area (liver, spleen) is cleared from the energies of Saturn. The Saturn frequency is replaced by the energy of Jupiter. Mars is attending the party to activate the process. The energies are positioned as follow:

Jupiter   Saturn

                          Moon

Mercury   Mars

Then, a pyramid appears (probably the Great one, in Egypt), with the combined energies of the Sun and the Moon at its summit. The vibration prepared in the past few months is beamed through the pyramid to merge with the vortex situated under the building. An explosion seems to happen, shaking the whole structure.

The Sanat Kumara, who has already started to vibrate with an extraordinary power/force bursts out of Light and Divine Joy. We would dare to say that he experiences a formidable cosmic orgasm. A new Era is starting, made possible by the combined energies of the 2 last eclipses super-exposing the vibrations of the Sun and the moon and using the Comet as a filter/booster.

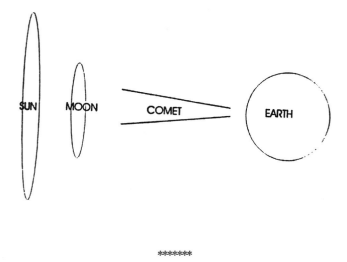

******

My life had taken a strange curve. Although, I did not want to leave this third dimension because of my family, everything in my life ended. Without really comprehending the implications of my decision, I started to write about 'MANIFESTATION' and one night, while sitting and praying, completely in her heart, I heard myself pronouncing these words: "NOT MY WILL, LORD, BUT THY WILL."

My personality is mainly a ray one, will, and this was perfect for the mission that I had committed to on the physical plane. I said:

"My God, whoever you are, I call upon you as the Heart and Consciousness of the Universes, as the only source of love and wisdom. Today, I promise to surrender and stop using my own wisdom, my own will, my mind power, and my ego. I will be supported by the flow of life, the flow of thy love. "Not my, My Lord, but Thine be done" (Luc 22,42).

Immediately, what a ride! It was better or worse, depending on your point of view, than Six Flags Magic Mountains! Within weeks, I had to let go of my activities, home. I was momentarily separated from my children. Fortunately, a family of friends, although in a different state, offered their home and love.

During the same period, I had stopped any work related to as- cension, to the refinement of the triangle pointed up. I was, on the contrary, bringing down my spiritual Self into the third dimension, in order to anchor more deeply my Monad into my body. Also, I was focusing on harmonizing my soul extensions, so that each expression of the soul would connect with the soul group and with the Monad.

Less than six months later, for the second time in this life, I was offered to leave planet Earth. I would say, more than a year later, that this is the way I heard the message through human perceptions, still living in duality:

" During a meditation, I received a full news broadcast, in Technicolor, transmitted to the team originating from the planet Sirius, of which a part my consciousness is very connected. Our work was to bring the DNA of Sirius to Earth and to incorporate our genetic system into mankind. The mission is completed, I can be back on Sirius!"

Well, great, although, I have been thinking about it for months, I react with anger and indignation:
-"What, are you crazy? What about my kids? NO, NIET."

By the end of February, I attend a workshop in which people learn how to draw their mandala. My intent is to spend two days in an art ambiance. In the morning, as soon as we close our eyes to meditate . . . here we go again, Technicolor and sound . . . I am in Egypt, above the great pyramid. The great priesthood, who originally came from Sirius to educate the human race, has completed its work and is leaving this vortex.

-"Ok. Ok, I got it, I am done, but my children are 12 and 14, so, thank you for the rubbish. Although, the human game has no more attraction for me, I have to stay."

I start painting, although I am not convinced that it is the easiest way to support my family. In the meantime, I use a materialization technique.

Some days later, at night, I attend a ceremony, on the subtle planes, during which hundreds of students come to honor me and say goodbye. In fact I was watching my own retirement party. For the new moon, I gave a workshop and felt that it was the last, although I am scheduled for Virginia and Washington in June. I announce to the group that I do not know where I will be in six months.

Then, through a dream, I learn that my karma with my genitor is finished. Free, finally. I wake up, fully conscious of the significance of this dream. "Timing is everything", as we say in English. It is difficult to go faster than the calendar, especially for a character like me, whose story is so intimately entangled with the story of humankind.

This is the end of the Pisces era, the Hierarchy with which I worked for thousands of years is leaving, the Masters are changing, the race is no more in the hands of the reptilians, the dragons of the old wisdom. As a Cobra, member of the Great White Lodge, ..., practicing inner Kabbalah and inter-dimensional geometry, guardian of the Light in the mystery schools, great priest in the Egyptian school, bringer of the science and genetics of the Blue Lodge of Sirius, teacher on the subtle planes, I have completed my mission. Or at least, I respected my commitments and served with this group and quality of vibration. I feel free from any spiritual agreement from the past.

But, if I try to use my mind to put all the pieces of the puzzle together, I miss something. The Hierarchy, who took responsibility for the Earth with Sanat Kumara, was under the influx of the forces of the 3rd planetary chakra, male in polarity. It is interesting to note that the masters, teachers, leaders of the past centuries were all polarized into male bodies. Except for my official character living in the United States, most of my extensions are male on Earth and androgynous elsewhere.

It is obvious, that, at an international level, women are emerging as leaders of the new frequency. Channels, writers, gurus, healers, they are coming in number and balancing the polarity of the race, of the world. The structures of the society are changing; the minds are getting ready for communities. Of course, we are not yet speaking about the majority of the population. For most people, spirituality is still an accessory, a hobby, but a great wave of disciples and initiates are appearing, with a beautiful level of consciousness, a heart filled with love, all devoted to serve God and the Hierarchies.

By the end of April, I feel so tired, that, in the middle of the night, I call the children's father. Exhausted, I am sitting on the floor, ready to die. Twenty-four hours later, my energy is back, but at 4 PM, I start shaking, from head to toe, without any reason. My jaws are clashing. I have no fever, I am not really cold, but I cannot control the phenomenon. My son turns the heater on, covers me with two blankets . . . no result. Finally, he decides to use energy. Normally his healing power feels like a storm . . . nothing . . . but I do not comment because I do not want to hurt him. My body keeps shaking for hours, and then I fall asleep.

When our friend Rudolph visits, some days later, my son tells him the story with a smile:

-"It was really strange . . . and then, when I magnetized her, nothing, it was empty!"

"Yes", was commenting my inner voice, just like when someone is dead. But, of course, I do not say anything to my son. Then at night, I wake up with a strange sensation. A voice is talking to me:

-"Look at the clock, this is important!"

I do so and go back to bed. For more than two hours, pieces inside my body are removed and replaced. I do not see anybody, even in clairvoyance, do not feel any hands. But I am opened, and pieces of about 18 centimeters square and one and a half-inch thick are substituted inside my body. I feel like a puzzle for toddlers, in wood.

It is almost Wesak (Buddha Festival, happening at the full moon of May). I look forward to celebrate, to fly to the Himalayas in my Light Body and meet with all my Brothers....

AND, SUDDENLY!!

A dove settles on a branch, three feet away from the window. As I write on the computer, she stares at me for a whole day. A subtle shift is occurring in my energies, while a voice starts speaking aloud in my ear. I perfectly know this voice, but this is the first time that it speaks so much.

"I AM the Christ Consciousness. We are One. I am Maitreya and you are Christ. I AM Maitreya. It is time to welcome Christ, the Christ Consciousness. It is time to embody the Christ, Maitreya, in your body. You are Christ, you are Maitreya.

The song does not stop.
"Christ Consciousness. Christ, Maitreya."

On the second day, the dove introduces her companion. On the third one, she brings friends....

Am I flying in the simplest expression of joy, integrating the Christ Consciousness or am I nuts? Also, I am strangely meeting people who introduce themselves as Saint Francis, Maitreya, Christ, the pope's wife...

And then, a lady who I just met, offers me two tickets for the Wesak festival in Mt Shasta. Do I finally have to rejoin the new age and spiritual community, and accept them unconditionally? It is difficult for me not to judge the New Age. The closest we are to Wesak, the more I feel in dichotomy. A part of me is euphoric while the other receives death sentences. I try not to think about it, and take homeopathic remedies for "Think of and predicts one's own death". No result. I have the sensation that it is urgent for me to finish my Mandala, on a canvas, as a signature, a testament . . .

Then, while organizing my travel to Mt Shasta, I hear:
-You will not come back after the weekend.

I prepare a legal document for the custody of my children and call some friends to say goodbye.

Crying, I say to Rudolph:
"Rudolph, I really think that I am leaving. You know that I want that, but it is cruel for my children. And, if I come back, I do not know how..."

Uncertain, I decide to speak to the children, without really saying what I feel, about the possibility of leaving the planet. However, I telepathically project this potentiality to their mind.

My Daughter, in the car, intuitively understands almost better than I do:
"You will have the same body.
-Yes.
-So, I will recognize you!"

My son does not even wait for a conversation:
"For Christ sake, stop acting like someone who is not coming back. You are leaving for a weekend!"
Here am I, in Mount Shasta. Although still on the defensive, I love meditating for several days. The attendees are beautiful, sometimes remarkable. The speakers are repeating: "Do not judge."

It is true that we are all wearing a costume, and that magnificent beings are hiding and serving behind that. From time to time the little voice speaks into my right ear.

On the morning of the full moon, I hike inside a cave, on Mount Shasta to do what I still call 'my real Wesak'. The Buddha enters the aura of the planet and meets the assembly of initiates, then the Sanat Kumara and the planetary Lords appear and join the assembly in meditation and contemplation. I am filled with gratitude. But one detail bursts my body with joy, when in my body of Light, I arrive in Tibet: my two children are already there and position each other on my sides. They are laughing, happy for such a good joke and shout out to me:

-"You know, Mother, whatever you do, we are here to support you!"

This is the first time that we have met for Wesak. I know that my son and daughter have both been receiving a special training for several months, at night, but I am still surprised!

******

May 21st, 1998

Ascension Day, forty days after Easter. A group of friends have invited me for a meditation. As soon as I close my eyes, I find myself on the other side, facing myself as Nora. If I was not yet convinced, it is time to face it. For 15 years, I have been, consciously, accompanying human brothers and sisters, after their death, to complete their purification, meet their family and the Light. I have no doubt about the place where I/she is.

She appears a little younger; her eyes pure and very clear. She is in peace, free from a burden that had become too heavy. I called for the end of this challenge; I called death, but was torn at the idea of two orphans. The universe gave me a proof of its intelligence, perfection and Love. This part of MySelf who was tired, who wanted to find her family again on Sirius IS BACK ON SIRIUS. Nora, as the part of my consciousness in charge of this body, left this planet on . . .

At the same time, a voice keeps speaking in my ear that I cannot ignore:
I AM GOD, I AM THE PRESENCE, I AM MICHAEL

During the weekend in Mount Shasta, the song is slightly different:
I AM the Light, I AM God, I AM Michael.

Although my life has always been anything but 'normal', I do not speak to anyone about my ongoing initiation, I feel strange, in contradiction with my belief system. But this voice resonating so deep inside me is so natural. In fact, I recognize it. This is the voice that I called 'Miss 911", because it only talked when I made the most important or urgent decisions of my life. I spend hours in a deep meditation, praying to incarnate my spiritual self, to anchor it wholly in this body.

Suddenly I realize that, for months, I have been praying and working for the integration of my spiritual self on the third dimension. My problem was not to be capable of travelling inter-dimensionally, to visit the Masters, to be Spirit, but rather to accept human life and manifest in the third dimension.

Therefore, several times a day, I exerted a pressure on my spiritual selves to anchor them down here. As often as possible, I inspect my structure and use sound, words, prayer, to stop any separation between Heaven and Earth. But also, I made a fundamental decision in front of the Universe and the Infinite Consciousness. For years, and probably because of the contracts I had as Nora, I had to use strength and will. No one incarnates with the mission of serving the planet by transmuting the shadow, no one is working for the Lodge and the Illuminati without a strong personality. And I admit that I/Nora was stubborn. But I finally SURRENDERED TO GOD'S WILL.

****

The house is empty. The children left with friends. After seven days of fasting, I do not really feel like attending the concert as I was supposed to. I only want to paint and meditate. The voice, very strong now and very precise of I AM, resonates in all my being.

Lord Michael speaks in English (Dear Readers, I am French):
-"Take four colors and spread them on the palette: Cobalt blue, Phthalo blue, white and black.

-Now, cobalt blue, some black, that's enough, put the brush on the top right of the canvas, relax, yes, like this, softly...

-Blue . . . white, a little more, a hint of black, go to the canvas, in the center, add some white, go to the right . . .

And so on, up to the moment a face and a personality are emerging, from a powerful blue background. It is not Rembrandt, but it is powerful and vivid.

-You will call it Blue Lightning."

When my son will come back home, he will exclaim: "Wow, this one, you will not sell it!".

******

MICHAEL: "Archangel associated with Hod and with the sphere of the planet Mercury. Associated with the South and the Fire."

-Michael, who are you?
  I AM Michael, ARCHANGEL OF FIRE,
  I AM the BLUE LIGHTNING

  I am the prince of the Darkness, the protector. I use the divine ray of faith.
  I preside to the Light and to the Darkness. I AM the transmutation and the fusion. I AM steel, gold and silver. I hold the dragon, because I AM the dragon,
  The dragon of fire, dragon of wisdom, the eternal principle emerging from the night,
  From the top of the firmament, I come back from a merciless battle with the dragon's fire.
  Fighting means to merge
  I fought, integrated the dragon to become the undifferentiated force
  I have no sex, no duality
  I AM THAT I AM
  I collide with the mountain and protect her
  I plant and destroy along the ravine
  I protect and chastise one who forgets his karma and dharma

I AM the multiple
I AM God
God has no form
No limit, no limitations
God IS LOVE
Love expresses itself indiscriminately according to one's purpose, one's destiny
When one feels chastised, rejected, it is that he himself rejected the secret mission of his heart and of his soul

I AM the One who arouses passion
The electric fire
The creating fire moves freely
It cannot be controlled by human mind
According to his own desires and agenda
My heart is in your heart
Your mission is to transmit the divine fire
You pass over souls like the eagle
You overshadow and sanctify them
You show them the path
Without object, without techniques,
You penetrate their core, cells, and change the path
Above the mountains, above the lakes, planes the Sovereign
You hear the chant of the springs
The song of the birds
All is harmony, no competition, no denomination
The concert of creation,
The concert of God
Does not ask questions
IT IS

Beloved,
Pray to rejoin my heart
Anchor yourself in the Blue Light and in my heart
Do not worry about your ascension, you already did that at 28.

The Holy Spirit overshadows you
Only center yourself on the divine force, the divine heart
Repeat those words, I AM THE LIGHT AND THE FORCE,
I AM GOD
You will feel this force more and more, then constantly within
you

I AM the God of the Darkness, because I conquered and
transmuted the darkness. I conquered the dragon of fire and
the dragon of wisdom.

What is frightening is the fire, the purifying and transmuting
fire
I AM the transmuter, the purificater

Darkness has no power over me
I AM the Light and you are the Light
We are One, One with Source
You are the Conscious Light
The Shekinah resides in you
Bring the Light in the temple of your body
Bring the Light to the human beings
Let the Dove come onto you
Pass through you to better reach the hearts

The Christ glorified, the Christ in the heart, married with
Spirit, Spirit sanctified by the adjunction of the heart/body
In the name of Iod, He, Vau, He, manifested by the addition of
Shin

I AM MICHAEL,
I AM THE BLUE LIGHTNING
I AM THAT I AM
SO BE IT. NOW.

****

I will add that, earlier in my life, I ignored the voice of my Monad, with whom I had always been in contact, because I did not know what the voice was. But when I disobeyed for the last time, I was aware that I increased my difficulties and pushed back the end of my karma of two years. Nevertheless, Lord Michael as well as the Beings with whom I am working on the inner planes, could not linger any more. Suddenly, I started to lose every watch that I would try to wear, and would say: " It does not only mean that our notion of time is almost obsolete. It also indicates that I have no more time, the Hierarchy announces to me that the time imparted is over."

At the time when my relationship with Lord Michael was still in the dialogue mode, He said, with an incredible amount of love and compassion: " I have been waiting patiently, Dear One, because of the immense love that I feel for you, for the being with whom I have been collaborating for thousands of years." Although I could not avoid laughing, realizing the amount of stubbornness that I had shown towards my Brothers of the Higher realms, I was most especially touched by the allowance, the compassion, the humility and the tone of this magnificent voice, my voice, that I will never forget.

****

ARCHANGEL GABRIEL:

I feel connected with the Beloved.
I AM THAT I AM
I AM the sweet heart of God,
I AM the sweet powerful Son of God.

Being the Son of God means that I represent and manifest

everything that He is, that He thinks, that He does, in perfect Oneness and happiness.

Beloved, my message for you today, is about obedience, the need to SURRENDER. Loving God, over all, means to surrender and, during the process, to forget all your desires, dreams, will, personal sense of knowing and enter a journey into the unknown and the impossible. For any human being, what God is going to ask seems unreal, untrue, and infeasible. But this is how we learn to create what human beings commonly call miracles. The mystery of God's creation still resides in ways that is far beyond human comprehension. God, His way is the way of the Spirit. You are still in the 3rd dimension, in matter, with the habits and thinking of matter. The shift that you are now integrating in your body is necessary. It is a time for erasing and then rebuilding your molecular thinking and belief system. Surrendering to rules or letting go of accepted common ones is to accept stepping into irrational behavior in order to allow the Universe to create for you in its own way or, to co-create what you design, for you, without effort, just by loving God. Isn't it easy and wonderful?

Although manifestation is not focused on third dimensional wealth, let us take the example of transmutation into gold that obsessed alchemists. You know John Dee (famous alchemist and hermeticist, advisor to Queen Elisabeth) very well, don't you? Well, this process is just a re-alignment of the internal structure. Same atoms, different configuration, different name. If you want to accomplish it, you first have to trust. No need of moon, ceremony, the old mysteries are gone and obsolete. Just look at any object with the wish into your heart, and feel yourself, not only as powerful as God, but AS GOD, the true LIFE FORCE. If you feel so, truly, without any doubt, if you are at-One with any part of the universe, then you can re-organize atoms, manifest anything. It is just, once again, the purity and the strength of the feelings, the determination to ascend to this frequency where you are ONE, the ONE and to RECOGNIZE it. To RE-COGNIZE is to "know or identify from past experience". As soon as you remember your origin, accept it and feel it at a cellular level, all is possible.

Pure JOY is one of the most important ingredients. Joy, happiness, serenity, coming from nowhere, just from the blessing of being alive and enjoying it. Creation rejoices the heart, but has as well to come from joy.

******

SURRENDER: ARCHANGEL MICHAEL/ MICHAEL

Beloved, I would like to use your story as an example. I am aware that you are still grieving and clearing memories from the past. I, Lord Michael, am here to work with you, but we also want to support and honor you.

Human beings do not really understand the significance of God's love. God is present to guide and support you, but you are expecting from God specific answers or ways that were taught to you by religions or by your family. The few who truly surrendered to God, often monks or nuns were/are considered special. No businessman would stop making plans, and only pray, in complete surrender to the Creator. In your case, you knew, since childhood, that your task involved much more than the physical dimension. You were conversing with God, with the Being that you called your angel-Myself-and were thoroughly guided. But you became stuck with a difficult challenge. Because of the sorrow, you asked me, Archangel Michael, to leave, until you would understand. This decision caused you a lot of tears, but because of the law of non interference, I, Lord Michael had to let you walk the path of solitude, and to add to the original Separation the isolation that you required.

Sometimes, Beloved, you might not understand God's path. You perceive the lessons that you decided to integrate as very tough. But, when an experience is too hard, it is because you do not see the open hand that you just have to change your point of view, or to surrender.

You only have to give your burden to God, to Us and you will have the solution. The more you use your own resources, the more you fight, the more resistance and pain you create: "I will greatly multiply thy sorrow, in sorrow thou shalt bring forth children." When a path is too hard, it is not God's will; it is that at a moment in time, you made a decision, and you are now under the consequences of this choice. Stop, Beloved, we pray you, stop being tenacious. DIVINE LAW is the law of SIMPLICITY and FLOW. We will add: if there is no love in your life, no easiness, make a shift. Pray to God and your Monad, invoke your guardian angel. Ask them to reveal to you clearly your role, where and with whom you are to be. Then, walk the divine path. If a project aborts, do not push. If the appointments are canceled or people are not collaborative, do not insist. Pray again and surrender to your soul.

When you were 16, you adopted the slogan "I want, I can, I must". Although, I repeat it, we are aware of the will you needed to carry your mission, you did not have to suffer that much. In order to have an easier path, you would have had to listen to the messages sent by your soul and your Monad. Also, because you refused to admit the shadow in the human being and because you were only looking at people as souls, you created difficulties for yourself by ignoring the human aspects of the others and then suffering because of it.

SURRENDERING to the Creator requires FAITH, TOTAL TRUST. And, we will add, when UNCONDITIONAL LOVE pervades, there is no more questioning. Love and faith co-exist.

Some of you Beloved, also have heavy karma to deal with. Although we use this term, do not sink into pain. We are not speaking about small personal power struggles, that you kept repeating over and over, beyond death and re-incarnations. We are here referring to commitments or spiritual responsibilities that you-all of our Beloved Brothers and Sisters in incarnation, created for yourself, with your own will. You used words, tainted with strong intent to seal oath and pacts. WORDS, especially charged with intent and emotion are a

PLEDGE. WORDS CREATE. In the past, you have created mystical orders, groups of initiates, brotherhoods. Because of the excitement of the moment, you chained yourself through rituals, magic, and commitments. You have sealed your present and future. No one can reach spiritual freedom unless he honors his word and complete what he started. Or at least, you need to make amends and honorably pay your debts.

In the present, the lesson is simple. You are remembering your true identity and you are very powerful. Now, pay attention to the way you are using your mind. Do not let it wander. Choose your words with awareness and love. Use the gift of speech with wisdom, carefulness and thriftily. Although we acknowledge the fact that you already let go of harsh, hurtful words, be subtler. Built your life by choosing correctly the commands that you give to the universe, to the elementals and devas, with your thoughts and word. Imprint, weave your life with frequencies of love, gratitude and joy. Imagine a home filed with the smell of warm baked bread and resonating with young laughter. This is the kind of atmosphere that you want to create in your life.

Regrets, judgements, limitations, doubt, incongruence, lack of love and confidence, competition, uncertainty, all these feelings belong to the past. These concepts, associated with the shadow, the third dimension, have to be progressively erased from your life. You are Lords and Masters, you are divine, behave as such.

I love you
IN LOVE AND LIGHT
I AM THAT I AM
LORD MICHAEL

******

PRINCIPLE #2—ACT ENJOY NOW

LAW OF NO TIME

The big lesson in life is to learn balance. Then, when one has surrendered his will to God's will, how does one manage his life in the context of the third dimension?

Although you are temporarily living in a body, one of the principles that will connect you easily with the subtle planes is the LAW OF INTEMPORALITY or no-time. Time only exists as a convention, to be able to understand and read the holographic movie of the third dimension. On the human level, the simplest way to apply this law is to live each moment intensely and in the NOW. Nothing exists, nothing is important except what I AM and what I DO NOW.

Think about it, about the extraordinary potentials of such a position:
-You do not create any anguish, depression because you do not fear the future. You do not anticipate in human projects, limited and imprinted with the vibration of the past. Your thought, is not an obstacle to the plan of the soul and the plan of the universe.

-Each moment is fully lived, with joy and pleasure. Your heart, your capacities to appreciate are fully open to participate in the dance of the energies and of the universes. This simple and tranquil serenity does not feed the emotional body but the heart, the soul. The emotional body is woven under the influx of the emotions generated by the subconscious mind, the desires and patterns of the past.

-Relationships with others are simple, direct, non-judgmental. You are capable of true attention. What is more refreshing than to know and to feel that your interlocutors are really listening without thinking about what you said or did last week, without anticipating their answer.

In fact, the art of living in the present is a form of perpetual meditation, because the mind does not wander and does not create new thought forms. The being is firmly anchored between Heaven and Earth, as a conscious part of the Whole, himself complete.

In practical terms, the disciple can simply live his life one day at a time. If he is connected with this Higher Self, he might ask every morning: "What am I supposed to do TODAY?". He can also let his intuition guide him or the voice of the Monad, KNOWING that he will receive instructions when the time is right.

Of course, each of you will have to adapt the answer to your own circumstances, their own lifeframe. If you are working in a multi-national company, it is obvious that this question will have several facets, although we believe that even a large company can become timeless.

If you have the courage not to depend on a fixed salary, the question is more open-ended. You commit to SERVE your SOUL, as a channel through which the creative force of the universe will express itself every moment, and without obstacles, thus in a magnificent, alive, constructive, loving way!

TWO PRINCIPLES are connected with THE LAW OF NO-TIME:

1. FAITH

A complete faith and deep love for the Divine are the sine qua non conditions to surrender to the Presence. When one cannot surrender, he is, in fact, introducing human conditions, woven with imperfection and instinctual fear.

Faith is the inner knowing, without any doubt that everything in your life is already taken care of, and that God only gives you the best. All the miasms, sin, separation, aging, disease, lack, challenges are then erased from your cellular memory.

2. THE UNIVERSE IS PERFECT—EVERYTHING IS PERFECT

The trust that you have in your own divinity, true faith, let you know, deep inside, that EVERYTHING IS PERFECT.

Whatever scene your body is playing, dealing with, now, in your small holographic universe, is a part of the perfect plan of the universe. The beings that you meet, their shapes, their faces, the colors that they are wearing, everything is perfect.

If you do not yet see or feel this principle deep down inside your heart, just keep it as a concept in your mind. You are a tiny piece of a grandiose plan of the Divine Consciousness, and yet you are as grandiose as the Whole, as you are the Whole. The only difference is awareness, consciousness, vision, which means, Dear Ones, that we are not separating or judging you, but yet, there is a challenge. Sometimes, it is not permitted for you to be aware of all your dimensions as a protection. It might be too stressful, too tough, confusing to be aware of or to remember everything that you do or are. For instance, you might be affected by a constant feeling of separation, that we would call the "I wanna go home syndrome", although there is no 'other' place or 'other home'.

The divine plan, although partially veiled to us does exist, unfolds and envelops you. Whatever happens, in your life, in the world, to you personally or to the community, is alive within God's breath.

The heart/mind of God beats at the same rhythm as yours, and you do not exist without this beat and it is not without you.

Therefore, you have no reason to wonder or worry. Your life is animated, IS because of the Presence, of the Divine Consciousness. You are an extension of this consciousness, you are God, and YOUR LIFE IS PERFECT.

Do not try to understand everything. Ask questions, but then, let yourself be guided. Spirit will answer. And, if you are under the impression that no response is coming, insist only being precise in your question. If there is still no answer,

-It is probably a question of timing. It is not time to receive this information or to start doing something.

-You do not need an answer. Eventually review the problem with a friend or a guide.

DO NOT BLOCK THE MANIFESTATION
—BE TRANSPARENT

The art of being neutral or transparent is one of the most difficult to practice: "Every man is tempted, when is drawn away of his own lust, and enticed." (James 1, 14)

You have heard these words many times, from the Christ, in the context of learning to control the basic instincts, such as sex, lies, theft, anything related to the first and second chakra. But, you might also apply it in reference to the addictions of your mind, to the daily drama that you decided to play in your personal movie, day after day, in the great theater of Malkuth.

Why don't you ask yourself these questions?

-What is the greatest challenge of my life?

-What situation do I expect to happen in my life, for a fact?

When one anticipates drama, he lives in a ball of wool. A thread without end is wrapped around you and the more you try to stop, the

more knots you make, don't you? A radical change of direction is
urgently needed.

During the convalescence period, the principles to follow are:
-Stop deceiving yourself, thinking that you are the master on board.
The commander of the boat is God and his assistant, your
Monad.

-Stop making plans, even to heal and especially to change the
situation. Your plans will undoubtedly be a new attempt of your
old personality to impose itself, with a slightly different
costume. All the principles on which your life is based are
obsolete, The third dimension is vanishing, do not try to bring
it back with your reasoning.

-Stop asking questions, even to God. The best mantra, if you need
one, would be: "I AM an instrument in your hands. Not my
will but thy will."

-    Completely stop your internal dialogue, whatever the content
is, your life, your health, others, or beautiful projects for the
future. The only acceptable words will be mantras, emotionally
felt and visualized, for instance: "I AM Christ, I AM the
Divine Presence." Or you might repeat the names of the
Masters or of Beings with whom you are establishing a
spiritual connection.

-Practice a meditative state as constant and as long as possible.

-When you speak, be very selective in the choice of words.

The Chinese have a very interesting way of illustrating the principle of transparency or neutrality. We refer here to the book "Rooted
in Spirit" from Claude Larre, SJ & Elisabeth Rochat de la Vallée,
translated in English by Sarah Stang.

"In the center, because of its position as a ruler, is the Heart . . . Happiness or unhappiness, illness or health, longevity or premature death all depend on the heart. The heart is taking the burden. The heart fills without knowing it. As soon as we are aware of this fullness, we must empty our heart. We must make haste to learn to unlearn, in order to reach non-knowing and to act only through non-action . . . The life of each being is authentic only insofar as it is carried by the natural movement that gives birth to the Ten Thousand Beings that are the radiant lineage of Heaven and of Earth. "

"Calm and quietude, the Art of the Heart, is not the denial of the movements and reactions that make up life. On the contrary, the Art of the Heart is in analysis of these movements and reactions. It is the temperance that distances anger and outbursts. It is the perpetual re-establishment of a balance."

DETACHMENT

If you truly sense the perfection of God's mind and have faith in the divine unfoldment of life, of your life, you will then effortlessly be DETACHED. When you dream or launch a wish, an idea, a project in the limitless infinite field of God's Love/Consciousness, you know that anything IS and just needs to be revealed before your eyes. And you also know, without any doubt, deep in your heart, that God only gives you what is best for you.

It is then easy to detach yourself from the idea, the thought-form that you tenderly laid in the nest of the universe's heart/mind. If you think that your life, your future, your happiness, your spiritual growth depend on the acquisition or solving or completion of your initial idea, then, you are only living on fear. The more you are emotionally needy or attached to the result of your quest, creation, the more resistance you generate.

When you believe in yourself as you believe in God, if you root

138 MICHAEL EL NOUR

your life in the now, you will release the habits of dwelling on objects, fame, and security. All these values, profoundly human, based on fear, and hopelessness are progressively replaced by the glorious feeling of self-love, trust and spiritual wealth.

On a practical level, when you have planted a seed, eventually done your third dimensional work related to it, then, release your attention, and surrender to the hands of the universe. The immense, powerful, wise, loving life force will work for you.

PRINCIPLE #3—SERVICE

I AM MICHAEL,
I AM THE LIGHT, I AM GOD

My purpose tonight is to explain how to serve.

The term service if often perceived as pejorative. Human beings refuse this vibration as a breach of their freedom, an alienation of the self by another self or a group.

But, in the logic of the heart, if it is possible to speak such a language, this context vanishes completely. We are all moved by unconditional love, and then by the aspiration of seeing our brothers and sisters grow and evolve in bliss. Our joy, our personal peace does not exist unless we know that our Beloved brothers are feeling well, have all they wish, especially spiritually speaking, and stand in divine awareness. This means that, as soon as we change our point of view, to be the servants of the Kingdom, the most important mission for us is then to bring the kingdom to the hearts of others. When you have experienced extraordinary, magnificent breakthroughs in your own life, you then appreciate and enjoy, with your heart, and instant after instant, the bliss induced by the fusion or at least the closeness of I AM. And you cannot, Beloved Ones, imagine living any more without the Presence, can you? Your reflex is then to do everything in your power to introduce the frequency of the Divine Presence in the life of a great number of souls. BEing, anchoring, sharing the GOD, DIVINE frequency is the most important part of SERVICE.

You now know, without any doubt, that each of you is a piece of the puzzle. I am here speaking of the immense weaving designed by the inhabitants of this planet, working as one at the manifestation of the magnificent scheme of Consciousness for this part of the galaxy and the role of earth in the history of the Universe. Your joy is increasing at the idea of serving the Creator. You want the others not only to experience the same happiness, but also to be ready to achieve their part. Then, more Light Workers having transmuted their frequency, assist Mother Earth, God and alleviate the Masters' and the Hierarchy's task. For centuries they have been working on the introduction of the millennium of light, which is the culmination of a cycle and of a story. Often times, the Masters wondered if they would be successful, for this part of the plan in this area of the galaxy, and according to God's schedule. They have been working zealously and without rest, sometimes guiding you like children, hand in hand. They taught you at night, assisted your meditations, initiations, patiently listened to your pain and complaints. The Masters also experienced life in matter and thus feel immense compassion for mankind. That is why it is now your duty to take over and assist others, around you, to see the reality of the Light and to BE it as fast as possible.

Serving does not necessarily mean to teach spirituality or meditation. Beloved, there are so many ways to contribute to the evolution of the race. Although the goal is ONENESS, and you are all ONE, each of you carry a personal vibration, and has his own practical manner to introduce this note/frequency to the planet and into the fabric of life. If all the initiates would scatter to all the areas of the community, more human beings would be touched. The educational system, the youth, television, media, the financial system, whether or not they will last, can and have to be enlightened by the presence of I AM. Some workers of the Kingdom enjoy the ability to travel. They are a connection between the groups emerging worldwide and are used as seeds. The DNA of the people that they are meeting is affected and set in resonance. Resonance, from heart to heart and aura to aura is now the most efficient and quickest instrument utilized by the Hierarchy to proceed to the mutation of the race. Because of the new physical and magnetic conditions of the planet, the law of resonance acts faster and in a more direct way than in the past.

Beloved, this is another reason to get into the ART of listening carefully to any impulse coming from within, from your heart. Do you suddenly feel like visiting friends? Do you think that it could be exciting to travel to your cousins, in a foreign country? Life might give you a little push. Do not resist. Let yourself be carried on by the intrepid, yet wise flow of the Infinite Consciousness.

Service is also the ability to give, freely, without expectation to others. It is not necessary to offer either expensive or material gifts. Sending light or love to a brother, to a planet, smiling to a stranger, listening, blessing silently a place, a town, an event are all facets of the loving art of giving. We know Dear Ones, that giving is already part of your life. However, some of you might be too busy or overwhelmed by human obligations. We thus recommend that you include this aspect of service in your daily life.

A very simple way to serve the Ascended Masters and mankind is daily personal practice. The more refined your consciousness is, the more clear your karma, the more you apply universal laws, the more you help Mother Earth to reach the vibratory rate now required for the globe and for humankind.

Thank you for your efforts, practice and Love.
We are with you, Beloved Masters.
I AM MICHAEL.

EXPRESS YOUR OWN GIFT

When the being is one with the Creator, in his heart and in his mind, he experiences the delights of bliss. Bliss is an inner feeling of joy, sweetness, contentment, completion, love and full realization of the self in oneness with God. It is the discovery of/and participation in God's own bliss of BEING, loving and giving.

If one can BE or center himself in this feeling, then his whole life is the simple, full expression of God himself.

Bliss into action is the capacity of the self to surrender, as a pure vessel to the natural, perfect flow of universal energy and love. This station in the center of God's heart/mind will create, whatever one's imprint is.

In fact, although we use the word action, the being is not the one who is initiating the action. There is no more need to do. The only effort, if there is some tension or strain going on, is not to do, perform, operate, but to keep ourselves into God's arms, in inner trust, surrender, centering yourself in the emotion associated with blessings. Then, bliss will spontaneously blossom into the right, perfect creation.

Bliss is such an enviable state. An unquestionable trust, pure detachment, true peace and serenity replace all of the extremes, all the feelings leading to sorrow, questioning, pain.

The right action, the right people, the right words will then manifest themselves without search, without effort. In fact, the PERFECT creation, IS already. Your only requirement is to align yourself with God and the creation will appear before your eyes, miraculously.

****

MICHAEL: EXPRESS YOUR OWN GIFT

A soul is a part, an extension of God himself, a reflection of the countless qualities and potentials of the Creator. The world, the universe reveals the diversity of life, the imagination, the power of the heart/mind of the universal sovereign.

You are a piece of a huge puzzle, which is the manifestation, in the third, or fourth dimension of God's thought and feelings. His projection is sent out as codes, a multitude of imprints, images that you are and that you carry.

Each of your qualities is God's gift to you and to any being who is part of the Universe. As a bearer of God's Thought, you have the responsibility to express the aspect of God that you are. By surrendering, you open yourselves to the flow of life and to the possibility of becoming aware of your BLUEPRINT. The blueprint is the magnetic encodement, the specific pattern that is embossed, impressed in our personal system/structure. Although we, you are all similar in terms of life force, and general physical appearance, each of you is the recipient of a unique aspect of the Creator's personality. God offered, without condition, a part of Himself, one or more gifts. This is what you are supposed to express. It does not have to be art or public exhibition. Your program, your affinity, the vibration you resonate with might be a sense of organization, raising children, or studying the stars. All of these tasks are complementary or necessary for the progress of the community. At an individual level, the important point is to feel comfortable in your work, and HAPPY TO BE in the body playing your part.

When one is living his blueprint, if you are a vibrant illustration of your soul, your path will be simple, easy, open and successful. You may want to ask your I AM to show you the way:

I, as my Divine I AM Presence
Stand centered in God's heart/mind.
One with the universe,
I express my divine blueprint
In the human dimension.

I am the manifestation of God.
I extend God's creation on the Planet.
SO BE IT. NOW.

IMPECCABILITY

ARCHANGEL MICHAEL:
Dear Brothers and Sisters, Beloved Ones:

It is with great joy that I AM addressing you today.

I am Archangel Michael, and I am here to support the force and strength that you all show in your spiritual work. At this time of great-accelerated changes in the deep structures of your planet, of your mind and bodies, we are requiring effort and attention from you all in specific areas.

Because of the implementation of the Bright, clear Light in this location of the body of the Logos, we are expecting a strong reaction from the forces known as forces of darkness.

Darkness is a word, a common human way to describe the inner balance necessary in the physical world. There is no fear, no consequences to feel or expect when one is putting his attention on the shadow. The shadow was the extreme expression of your physical dilemma, which is now disappearing with great speed. The velocity and sudden increase of the brightness of your energies, the wonderful work that you are and have already accomplished may trigger, for reason of habits and balance, a wave of difficulties among the Light Workers and the people of the new nation.

We are asking you in order to help your devoted oldest Brothers to accomplish their mission, which is to accompany you, dear beloved and the planet to the Light, to ACT PERFECT.

Perfect, means to constantly focus on your HIGHEST, best THOUGHTS, to harness your mind so that no struggle, or interferences will be created from each and all of you, which would require more work and attention from the others and from us, your dedicated assistants.

Do not allow your minds to wander on the past, to worry, and to create any more reflection of the old ways. Do not allow your minds and hearts to weaken. We are asking you to be warriors over your own last pieces of human, alienated consciousness. Be aware of any action, or thought that you might entertain or play out, just because it has been your old, normal way. Be aware of the new vibration dispensed in your magnetic field by your Lords and High Brothers to help you change yourself at a cellular level.

Any tool or any assistance that you require is sent to you magnetically. Just plug yourself in this magnificent wave of Light, which is over your planet. This is no time to look for a new type of meditation and a new teacher. We understand your needs for mental structures and techniques, your admiration for the old helpers still in a physical body. But all these are products of the past, miasms that you have to identify and clear.

While looking at yourselves, Beloved Sisters and Brothers, please do not hurt yourselves by lack of COMPASSION. Just watch, witness the process of your minds and body and acknowledge it. Then release it and ask your I AM presence, your Godself, to REPROGRAM your CELLS in harmony with the PURE BLUEPRINT of the LIGHT and the pure encoding of the Universe, the ALL IN ONE.

Compassion is a key that comes with practice. Compassion has been forgotten, neglected in your world, a world where the warrior mentality is still prominent. It is not necessary to be harsh on yourselves, just set yourselves in the flow of God's immense unconditional love. Just lay down, spiritually speaking, in God's arms, with the candor, trust, confidence of a new born baby, looking in his mothers eyes, and resting, floating in her loving arms. A new born baby, what you are right now in terms of your evolution on the planet does not ask himself any questions, does not worry about his next meal. He is a full expression of purity, clarity, trust and love. Bear in mind the words of our Beloved Master, the one you know as Jesus : "Let the children come to me...". A child, a baby, does not hate himself because of his body, because he needs his mother's help and attention to change, wash and feed him. He lives naturally, candidly, at one, with the family that he chose, knowing that everything is already taken care of, by the universe.

Let's go back to your daily path, your actions. Be IMPECCABLE. We repeat, impeccable. Although we emphasize on the balance of self-compassion and rightness, we are requiring great effort from you. Live your highest frequency, your highest life, your highest hope. DEMONSTRATE DAILY your ATTACHMENT to the PRIN-CIPLES of the HIGHEST PURE LIGHT. Do not allow yourself to hesitate between your old personality, your old patterns, and the manifestation of the Dove. PRACTICE, as the MASTERS that you already are, in your body. You are Masters, you are the I AM GOD, incarnated and engaged in a trip into matter. Allow yourselves to remember who you are, to AWAKEN the CODES to mastery and WHOLENESS.

No exterior intervention is necessary. Although you can use many tools or sounds. The most powerful, sweet sound is the one of your own deity, godness, seeded deep in the core of your Being, in your heart.

It seems important to emphasize on the subject of your impecca-bility. We might sound a little archaic, a little fatherly, but some do not live and express themselves at the best of their capabilities. Im-peccability is a way to create more Light, to anchor an intent, a higher frequency, which will balance any attempt of the darkness to slow down the process of ascension of Mother Earth and of Mankind.

PURIFY your DAILY ACTIONS. Old patterns of lies, duplicity, greed, competition, control, separation, addictions, are to be released. Do not feel guilty if this requires some time and some challenges but set your mind, your intent, to be always at your highest behavior, practicing the fruits of pure love and God's perfection. Do not let the old ways pull you away from your goal, RE-ENLIVEN and MANIFEST GOD, in your BODY NOW.

Give yourself enough time every day to contact and rest in the beauty and strength of your I AM Presence. That is to say, allow yourselves to access, feel and RE-ACTIVATE the PARADIGM of LIGHT, UNCONDITIONAL LOVE, and WHOLENESS.

I Am Michael, your servant, your Lord.

I AM Michael, your protector, the carrier of the blue ray, the rider of the dragon, in the heart of God. I AM Michael, your brother, yourself, an expression of the infinite mind of God. Be blessed, Beloved, and receive the Bright Blue Light. I AM THAT I AM.

* Note: Although this was a personal message, we think that other beings assuming the role of parents will like to read it:

A word for the little ones: We love your children. Keep them safe, by the love that they will feel every day, along the path. Children are open-minded; they are not yet as judgmental as adults are. Instruct them of the ongoing changes. Children are now receiving a special attention from the Masters. They are tutored and re-programmed during their sleep. Notice how open they are to the new paradigm of Light, to any invention, any change. They are the ones releasing all the old programming of the world. They already are the future. Honor and cherish them as the seed of future.

Be prepared to jump into the new dimension with them. Prepare your mind and body. Embrace them with love and set your eyes towards an expanded idea of the world, where you will carry the vision together, in unconditional love, oneness, and expansion.

PRINCIPLE #4—LOVE

I AM THE BLUE ANGEL, I AM ARCHANGEL MICHAEL

MY PURPOSE is to transmute, through the fire, any feeling into the pure vibration of the divine, into the pure vibration of Love.

Unconditional love explains itself. It is easy, Beloved Ones, for those of you who have children to understand love, especially for the mothers. How does a mother love her children? Immensely, blindly sometimes, unconditionally.

Do you keep a record for the flesh of your flesh, the blood of your blood? Do you write down their weaknesses and deceptions? No, you even forget their punishment, when you try to make the decision to teach them a lesson, don't you?

Well, God is our Father, and the Earth, our Mother. They are here for us, at any moment, for anything. We just have to remember it and to believe it.

Only the son and daughter can make the decision to leave the family. The core, the heart, does not cease to exist. The family waits, IS. The bondage between the members of a family IS.

Your difficulty is in loving others. It is in remembering your origin. When one remembers God, before the separation, when one is back to wholeness and oneness, LOVE IS.

Therefore, your challenge is to love yourselves. The conditions, the stones between you and your brother are only the stumbling block still existing in your consciousness. This is the reason why you bring them to you, manifested, under the disguise of another human being or a situation.

DO NOT JUDGE, anyone, any situation. I repeat, firmly and with tender compassion, everything is perfect.

All of the principles, all of the laws of the divine are condensed into love. You surrender because you love. You enjoy, trust, serve, give yourself, practice integrity, because you love. Even when you do not know why you love, let God take the burden and guide your steps.

Discernment is reserved for the wise man, to the heart that is already detached. Otherwise, even discernment is parenting, giving yourself, under any pretext the right to utter your emotions, and keep them away from another being, from yourself.

When you have to make a decision, about your brother or sister, and you feel judgmental, place your attention in your heart, send love to the other being, and bless the challenge that he or she, or you are going through in order to understand something. The real story, as you know it, happens on other levels. Maybe this being is here to bring out and transmute an aspect of Mother Earth or an aspect of the shadow that he/she took responsibility for. In this regard, accompany your brother in his courage to carry his task. If you feel hurt, it may be that he is carrying a part of your shadow. In this case, why not do it together?

If you need to momentarily move away from another being, examine your heart; is it about power, recognition, self-doubts? Follow your emotions; do not try to explain. However, even following your deepest feeling, the voice of your intuition, remember that anybody still dealing with these questions is definitely still under the veil of self-discovery.

The being who already transmuted and installed himself in full, unconditional Divineness, Godness, is detached. There is no question, no situation of separation. Judgement and questioning are evidence of the necessity to keep working.

God IS, GOD IS LOVE, LOVE IS GOD.

The second word, "unconditional", is already a trace of humanness, impurity.

Beloved, this also applies to our relationships with ourselves. Stop trying. BE. Forget the others, forget the work, be God and you will feel love growing in your heart. Make God your best friend, your permanent date. Be with him, to become him, LOVE.

SO BE IT, NOW.

A STORY FOR THE YOUNG HEARTS:
In the beginning there was Love, Love extended Himself . . . Love positioned himself on the other side, as a mirror. And love started to question. The first question, the first doubt: "Who are you?" Love was unfamiliar with having a mirror to watch himself with. Love answered, from the mirror: "Beloved, I am you". But the voice was different, reversed. How was that possible? This was the second question. Love decided to open his eyes, differently, and to investigate. Love started to travel, faraway, out of himself, towards, into the mirror...

LOVE

It is difficult for Human beings, because of their feeling of separation to grasp the significance of God's love. God is always present to guide and support you, but you are expecting answers or directions from God to be the same as the ones taught to you by religions or by your family.
SURRENDERING to the Creator requires FAITH, TOTAL

TRUST. And, we will add, when UNCONDITIONAL LOVE pervades, there is no more questioning. Love and faith co-exist.

Bliss is an inner feeling of joy, sweetness, contentment, completion, love and full realization of the self in oneness with God. It is the discovery of/and participation with God's own bliss of BEING, loving and giving.

When you align yourself with God's heart, you place yourself in the natural flow of Divine Love. Love is the key to any realization, relationship, manifestation, and abundance. It is the cement of the universe, the glue, let us say a very soft one.

******

Deep in the nest of my being
Is a shivering
A smile of my cells
An opened hand
A quietness
A certitude

A constant praise
For you, Beloved mirror
Beloved reflection of Myself
Beloved body of God

An endless prayer
To the radiance
Of the multiple faces
Of the creation

An everlasting gratitude
For my being a part
Of this incommensurate
Breath of God

Deep in the core of my core
Which limit is the Infinite
The boundless Universes
Is a blooming rose

Gods' love, my love, LOVE

I AM Archangel Michael
And I wish to speak tonight, Beloved Ones, about the path of
Love, and first the path to Love.

Although you are God, which means that you ARE Love, you
do not remember. This is the reason why we sense that we have to
learn again, to become innocent again.

Is innocence possible after sojourning in the bowels of the
Shadow? Is it imaginable to be back to our child essence after merging the self with the facets of the internal world, with all the faces of
dragons, demons and incarnated fear?

Yes, Beloved, just trust, abandon yourself, let go of the mind. These
are all only the disguise of the mind. In times, it had a purpose. In the
image of God, you created a reflection, a thought, a journey. It is time to
come back, to inhale, and to feel the immense heart of the infinite.

Just accept to consider rest, bliss, and beatitude as possible. It is
yours. It is the divine gift, waiting for you, waiting for acceptance to
receive.

****

Each time I feel this sweet vibration
Flowing gently within my heart
And inundating my body my limbs
Of deep calm and happiness

And no question

When I welcome any creature any experience
With a deep feeling of gratitude
Looking at God through the eyes of the living
Through the embrace of facts, situations
And no question

Whenever I greet and adore anything anybody
With a sense of recognition
A smile acknowledging the beauty
The magnitude, the intelligence, the hidden moon
And no question

When I acclaim life with an equal breath,
Without a wave in the ocean of my being
Without a storm in my inner night
In such a deep peace and serenity
And no question

When my laugh rejoins my cries
In a unique sense of Oneness
With any feeling, joy or pain
Shared with others, with the world
And no question

When I AM, in full certitude
Doing what comes on the moment
In full bliss, as the perfect act
As the highest accomplishment
And no question ever

I know, that Love is on its way
I know that I AM, in Love.

I AM Michael

PRINCIPLE # 5—
DIVINITY AND ONENESS

I AM PRESENCE—LOUD
INTRODUCTION

I close my eyes and ask my Divine I AM Presence to incorporate my physical temple. A cross of Light appears above me and slowly enters my body. In its center an ethereal form emerges, white and golden, as a Christ of Light. This being (part of my being, to be exact), his arms slightly extended, open, with a refined face, soft and strong, filled with compassion and an extraordinary love, is Me, my I AM Presence and is anchoring itself again in my heart. I am suddenly inundated with joy, peace, love, and happiness, everything at the same time. It is so unique and deep that my eyes are tearing. My skin, my cells sparkle like champagne. Happiness is back, simple joy of the return home, the true, ultimate return to the womb of the Divine Consciousness.

******

I AM GOD, I AM THE LORD

What are these words expressing when they naturally ring at the marveled disciple's ear?

The magnificent Presence, the I AM finally appeared; the last veils of human illusion are torn. The traveler has finally recovered his true identity. For years he had been wandering in a spiritual desert, experiencing hunger and thirst, solitude, exile. Physically free from slavery, as the Israelites from Egypt, his spirit guided him beyond the limits of the mental plane, to a deeper search, more extra-ordinary.

A mental decision to stop being a slave, which is to let go of the past, is not enough. The treasure hunter has also to refine his heart, to affirm that nothing is more important than to find God, without condition, without questions. This is why, when he thought that he had found freedom, the secret of God's blessings, he finds himself wandering in the desert for forty more years. Why? To understand that the Lord of the Universe, God and only God can show him the way out of the desert. The mortal individual suffers from being separated from God. His trust and faith are tested every day, patiently, so that, the being, purified by fire, becomes ONE with his soul, ONE with God, ONE with the WHOLE. Then it is time for the Presence to incorporate itself in the human costume, to enter the temple finally duly cleansed.

The being understood and demonstrated, daily, that the liberation of the body, of the third dimension, that is to say contingencies inherent to the physical plane have nothing to do with intelligence, culture or mathematics rules. Freedom occurs when one abandons all for innocence and purity, by the Baptism of the heart. The treasure that he looked for, in vain and often in tears, was there, in front of him, in him, in his heart, where the Soul dwells, the connection with the Whole.

The brain learns, understands, deducts, and builds. The Soul, via the heart, feels, emotes, and loves. The primary home of the being evolves through time, climbing the following steps:

1.   I exist through instinct
2.   I exist through the other, inter-action, re-production
3.   I exist through strength, power, conquest, domination
4.   I AM through love, the heart
5.   I AM and express myself through Creation
6.   I AM and communicate with the Divine Whole
7.   I AM THAT I AM

When the seeker crosses the first three doors or initiations, he starts feeling the opening of the heart chakra. The seed is planted. He is from now on in contact with his Higher /self, with his Soul. He loves the other and himself enough to be touched by the Divine Spirit, but IS not I AM yet. ANAHATA, the heart center is partially open. The process started when the cardiac lotus turned itself upwards (See I AM THAT I AM, ALTA MAJOR). The terrestrial triangle, ascending, material, is built. The being then works the energies of the centers five to seven and prepares the descent of Spirit, symbolized by the triangle pointed down. Finally, when the two forces are balanced, they progressively become interlocked with each other. The center of gravity of the individual is now established in the heart. The seed, planted by the student in the past, has blossomed. Anahata is not only struck, as the heavy doors of the old homes of the past, with a knocker. The heart IS HOME. *(Anahata means unstruck). The being is complete. He united the male and female principles, temporal and timeless, material and spiritual. He is reborn, Whole, through the heart. He is Divine, he is God. I AM. I AM THE PRESENCE.

The phase of awareness through the mind is over. The individual feels, IS. Through Co-birth*, he is co-creator, Master of his universe and his destiny. The voice of I AM finally reaches his ear. Literally he hears, not only the music and sounds of the infinite creation, but the voice, accessible to the human ear, of the Presence. This voice guides and marvels him; he bathes in God's aura and feels the return to the Womb of the Universe, the ecstasy and bliss, inherent to completeness and union. The Presence now anchors itself in the temple of the body, at a cellular level. The time required depends on the person and especially their capacity to let go of the old self and of the subconscious mind.

When the Divine Presence overshadows, merges with the individual, the voice of I AM can be perfectly audible, so that no doubt will remain in the mind of the applicant. Some, when it happens, who are already gifted with intuition, healing abilities, clairvoyance and clairaudience, will keep these tools as long as the soul needs them.

However, the appearance of I AM in the body is an initiation. The gifts guiding the New Born in Spirit may disappear. Why? Because the Presence is refining itself in the physical vehicle and becomes the PRESENCE IN THE HEART. Nothing more is necessary to guide the soul than the vision and voice of the heart, consequences of a perfect sensation, BEINGNESS AS the divine. If I AM GOD, my voice is God's voice. The phases of self-awareness and growth are:
-Attraction
-Intellectual knowledge
-Intuitive apprehension
-Sensation
-Being, I AM.

Let us go back to the time of initiation. The Presence introduces itself, joyfully, and eventually loudly. The change is sometimes so deep, that the subconscious mind lets go over night. The individual is blessed with a period of ecstasy so that he will witness and feel, in his own flesh, the blessings which are the results of the renunciation to and of his ego, the advent of the Christ and of the Presence. Literally held in God's arms, the being lives now out of the world and out of time. He is instructed about the reasons of this miracle. The principles of I AM are taught to him and explained. After several weeks or months, I AM firmly dwells in the heart. The being, restored in his divineness, walks through the heart, instructed by the voice of the heart. He does not need any longer to be guided through miracles-according to human understanding. HE IS, THUS HE KNOWS. His inner knowing, intimate awareness, certainty are now his path.

The loud expression of I AM is felt as a time of exultation. Who did not battle with old thoughts and programming? What a blessing when the internal dialogue is suddenly replaced by the soft, melodious, loving, perfect voice of I AM.

During the intermediary phase or gestation, I AM manifests itself in a more subtle way. The individual is still free, he has the choice. He experiences both states, the imperfection of the domain of the subconscious mind and the perfection of the divine plane. I AM has to anchor itself to the point that the tissues and cells are modified. The old programs might reappear like old ghosts. With compassion the Beloved new bearer of I AM is advised to observe, witness the phenomenon, accept, without judgement. The old patterns will slide away.

Also, while the Presence is progressively becoming integrated and silent, do not feel low-spirited. It is the right time to humbly turn to the Infinite Consciousness and incorporate this new step in your growth. Although each of you is unique, here are some ideas:

-An initiation, the passage of a door is a moment. After the portal, a new quality of vibration was definitely anchored in the multi-dimensional structure. Major initiations are given by the Lords at specific times, like the Wesak ceremony. All the seekers, ready for a reward or graduation receive their diploma when they are touched by the rod of initiation, or instrument transmitting the flux of energies of the initiators. This moment is often marked by, what we would call a small miracle, that you will remember all your life. Afterwards, the daily routine is back. The benefits and growth consequent to this new frequency are progressively processed and manifested in the life of the disciple.

-Gifts or spiritual capacities are not a proof of evolution. They are used for a specific purpose, temporary or not, and are not to be viewed as a power, a demonstration or a door to the Divine.
-Faith or total confidence in the raison d'être of any situation, understood or not, is the sine qua non condition for a fast and constant alignment with God.

As a gift of love, the Universal Consciousness may, through its 'loud presence' offer a period of grace. The initiate has a demonstration of the perfection, harmony and love flowing and nurturing the world. He feels completely loved, supported, protected as long as he stands as ONE with the Presence. His daily life is pure bliss, a stream of blessings, and he feels the benefits generated by TOTAL FAITH.

Then, as the Presence dwells silently in his heart, the new initiate is facing a new challenge. Will he still proclaim and embody the perfection of the universe. Will he walk, happily, although he does not know where and for how much time? Will he stay centered in his heart?

****

NAME AND UNITY

I AM MICHAEL
I AM THE DIVINE LIGHT
I AM THAT I AM

When God revealed Himself to Moses, he did not introduce his divine presence with a name. A name is an expression of individualization or separation from the peaceful universal consciousness. Sounds are tools, an emanation at midway between God's Spirit and form. Sounds project, transmit a vibration. The words and specifically the names appeared when the mind and discrimination were introduced in the sphere of creation. In the Bible, the story is translated as such: Adam was created by God and Eden was his home. "God brought the animals unto Adam to see what he would call them." Adam then recognizes the presence of different beings and identifies them outside of himself."

When they are speaking to human beings, your spiritual brothers are using a denomination or a color in order for you to recognize or identify them. However, they often use, at the end of their transmission the same words: "I AM THAT I AM". When he revealed Himself to Moses, God or the Being who is introduced as God, also says: I AM THAT I AM.

In fact, by those words, all of God's emissaries recognize symbiosis, UNITY, their belonging, with the Whole. Not only did they remember their Divine nature, but they fused into perfect osmosis into the Whole and are undifferentiated.

Your need to identify yourselves, to make statements about yourself is only the demonstration of your own doubts about the intrinsic nature of God and your capacity to unite, to identify yourself to the ONE CONSCIOUSNESS, limitless and formless, a so great and absolute concept that you are frightened.

When one belongs to the Whole, he has access to the Universal Wisdom and ceases to have to justify or prove what he is or what he believes.

If you KNOW, within your cells and blood, you are no longer looking for differences, which is a form of separation, because you recognized the aspects of the Whole, as the All in One, that you are.

SECTION III

HEAVEN ON EARTH

1. DEFINITION OF MANIFESTATION

What we encourage you to develop is the telepathic communication, the self-opening to refined senses to the point of being an empath. The goal is not to receive information, but to open yourself in order to unite with others, with the Whole. It is the acceptance of being and therefore supporting any other person, any part of the creation as yourself. It is sharing your brothers' and sisters' challenges and experiences as yours.

Ascended Masters, Angels utilize telepathic imprint in a very simple way. You ask yourself a question and perceive the answer, as inner awareness, inner cognition. After a period of training during which the candidate learns to listen, develops self-confidence, you will receive innate knowledge in the areas you are interested in and connected with your mission/blueprint. If you have dedicated your life to serving God and the Hierarchies, you will receive precise messages about the work to do or simply the places to visit. Loud clear audience is not necessary. The more refined you are, the easier you will hear the messages of the heart.

*****

Manifestation is not just a personal, selfish achievement of co-creation in your own life or universe, it is not just individual ascension. It is the total, unconditional acceptance and participation in God's will, manifested through a plan, a scheme. God is completing a circle, through which He feels and expresses Himself and you do it, ARE it, simultaneously.

On a practical level, whether or not you have remembered your divineness does not change the fact that you agreed to incarnate. By doing so, you accepted to be encoded with a mission or to be built to do/be something specific. This does not mean that all Christ soldiers have to be renowned leaders, inventors or the new planetary Christ. Your task might be to carry the Christ and divine frequencies and to make them available to your family, friends, and anyone who will cross your path, guided by the flow of life.

In the vast scheme of the universe for the planet, light workers have been sent as emissaries in this system to lead earth to a definite and unique level of evolution or vibratory rate. Each received one or more gifts, according to their genetic encodement. It is now time to embody those aptitudes or talents in order to complete the plan. This is how you manifest an aspect of Universal Consciousness, a facet of Divineness. In fact, we are all gathered to demonstrate and witness, in matter, the greatness, beauty and love of the Divine Consciousness. Therefore, when one attains alignment and harmony with his soul, as a divine self, he is ready to represent God. Divineness, inner peace, joy, a smile on your face or the love that you broadcast are the simple tools used by God to manifest Himself, to be.

In practical life, manifestation is:
-The manner in which you raise your family, the way you speak and behave, your level of faith and integrity.

-The health of your physical body, as a result of balanced cellular and organic functions married with self love and love for your life.

-The love that you demonstrate for Mother Earth, the wisdom and respect that you confirm in your behavior towards nature and the environment.

When each and all of you are dedicated to manifest God, when you all ARE God, the ALL IN ONE, then Heaven is projected on

Earth, and the paradise promised by the Christ is established. God's and Christ's kingdoms are implanted on earth according to the phases as stated below.

-Dream, prophecy
-Intuition or intuitive comprehension of the kingdom
-Seed planted in the heart
-Presence in the heart
-Exteriorization or materialization

1. DREAM, PROPHECY

The being hears about the Kingdom or about the effects of the Kingdom on people and society. In fact, the Kingdom being a state encoded in your genes, you carry the dream and hope, even unconsciously. Prophecies, myth are the keys that are opening the code, the awareness.

2. INTUITION

Although you might not know precisely how the Kingdom has to be established on the planet, you have the intuition of the blessings generated by the manifestation. Periodically first, you feel and experience spirit in your heart and in your life. You know then that it is the secret of happiness and inner peace.

3. THE SEED PLANTED IN THE HEART

You have achieved enough work on the spiritual level, roughened down your structure to the point of opening the heart chakra. A situation, a meeting, will create the advent of Christ in the heart. You understand that the purpose of life is to find God. You make the inner decision to consecrate yourself to your growth, to find the keys, to cultivate Spirit. In fact you change your orientation and polarity. You are no more a human being, focused on material vanities. The divine seed is planted in the right soil.

4. PRESENCE IN THE HEART

You merge with the Christ Consciousness and with I AM or the DIVINE PRESENCE. You are divine, you are God. From now on, your soul or more exactly your Monad lives and expresses itself through an individual, you. More than being intuitively felt or understood, The Soul is alive. Descended in the third dimension, it is integrated in your structure. THE DOVE IS ALIVE IN THE HEART OF A HUMAN BEING. GOD IS.

5. MANIFESTATION

God expresses Himself on the human plane. He creates and manifests. The being, you, are the master of the third dimension. You mastered the physical plane. Integrated and open to the flow of Consciousness/will and Divine Love, the Heart/Mind of God, you are a part, a channel, and an expression of the creative, vital force of God and the Universe. As God, you express the Universal Laws, you are being trained to create your own universe:

MANIFESTING THE CODES

You are in peace, in alignment in your structure, in harmony with your raison d'être. You are thus affecting individuals, groups. Consciously or not you will be sent or attracted to events/people. Your presence is enough, your energy modifies the course of the events in aligning it with the universal plan. The amplitude and rapidity of your action depend on' your capacity to stay centered in the flow of God's Consciousness.

You might be programmed to operate through a profession, religion, political party, a group, a hobby or just your friends. The Ascended Masters are often utilizing people in silence, although their impact is obvious through God's eyes. The initiate might be receiving the impulse from the Hierarchy to work on reforming the society, the laws. You might also introduce new patterns, colors in daily life through architecture, fashion, art. Musicians introduce the rhythms and tones that are necessary for the moment.

MANIFESTING THE FRUITS OF SPIRIT

The reform of the thought process, and then inner self-transmutation lead the individual to manifest the feelings inherent in unconditional love and perfection: joy, peace, faith, confidence, trust, abundance, etc. Your radiant presence sows the seeds of love everywhere you are. The people that you meet notice your inner beauty, the beautiful unfolding of your life, and moreover, they receive the divine message from aura to aura. Telepathically or by osmosis, others' frequencies are modified.

PHYSICAL MANIFESTATION

-Completion of projects
-Art
-Inventions
-Healing, molecular transformation

THEORY, HYPOTHESIS OF THE MANIFESTATION, EXTERIORISATION OF THE HIERARCHY

With abundant patience and compassion, the Ascended Masters and Spiritual Brothers introduced themselves to humankind. Although the majority of the population is not obviously affected, thousands have heard the call and in the next few months the Christ Consciousness and the Divine Presence will overshadow thousands.

FROM CHANNELING TO EMBODYING

The communication techniques utilized by the Ascended Masters and spiritual Brothers have been evolving according to times, necessities and to the growth of humankind. The presentation of the message is also adapted to the progress of the masses. In the past, it was imperative to strike the consciousness by incredible revelations or events considered miraculous. The population, mostly illiterate, more superstitious than spiritual, uninformed, would respond to prophets, magicians, psychics or oracles.

At the great turning points in history and the formation of new races, Spirit used fantastic events to strike human's consciousness, such as the arrival of extra-terrestrials seen as semi-gods or tablets written by God's own finger.

The twentieth century and especially the last two decades have been marked by the emergence of hundreds of channels. The Ascended Masters, Christ, Melchizedek, unknown beings by the dozens introduced themselves to give you messages, from the simplest to the most phenomenal.

We do not give credit to all the channels as being really in contact with the Ascended Masters or the being they refer to. Unfortunately, many are only communicating with deceased, astral spirits, extra-terrestrials with selfish, hidden motives. Belonging to a non-human plane is not evidence of spiritual evolution. Many humans confuse mechanical or technological advances with spiritual wisdom and enlightenment.

When you open a gateway, by responding to extra-terrestrials and creating a group, therefore an egregore (mass, energy-form, thought form created by a group of people thinking in the same direction, using the same prayers), you are carrying their frequency on the planet and you are responsible for the consequences. When a powerful entity uses you to anchor his personal power, whether or not the information given to you is true, you damage your health and carry an unnecessary burden on yourself. Also, all of these interferences are complicating the task of the Hierarchies and of the Conscious Light in assisting Mother Earth in her ascension.

The positive aspect of this experience, if these channels are not spiritually and physically affected or harmed, is that they are learning telepathic communication, self-confidence and are therefore growing through the process.

A number of channels are truly in contact with high beings, or at least with an aspect of them. This method of communication allows the spiritual brothers' awareness and frequencies to be conveyed to humankind. Also, the channels have understood that, any individual, in alignment and harmony with his own Higher Self, or I AM presence accesses more refined frequencies and information.

******

How is the Hierarchy going to project itself on Earth? Can you imagine the Ascended Masters, the Archangels walking down among you? This would imply the reconstruction of a body in which spiritual beings would be subject to the limitations of matter and of the shadow. Their vehicle could appear and disappear spontaneously on the earth ground, but their power and freedom, acquired through evolution and transcendence would definitely be affected. On the other hand, the Spiritual family, the Ascended Masters have responsibilities to fulfill on the subtle planes and in the Cosmos.

The graphic on the next page gives a very simplified idea about the creation and apparition of the race on planet earth. We do not pretend to reveal, in one paragraph, the whole mystery of creation because we are still in a physical body, thus living in the veil of matter, and subject to personal interpretation of any information. Nevertheless, we are offering our own experience and thoughts to the Beloved readers: The Universal Consciousness did not create, per se, each of the Monads inhabiting the Universes. God extended Himself to the exterior. He manifested other beings or energy forms that are his direct sons. These sons are the Creators or Gods who have been invited to duplicate the phenomenon of exteriorization. Each creator IS and holds his own signature, in the sense that he is an aspect of the Universal Consciousness and he re-produces this specific frequency.

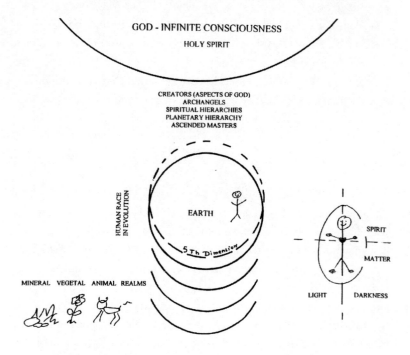

RAY FACTORS

Each human carries a ray or major vibration, the ray of the soul, corresponding to the chakra of the Being or Logos to which he is linked. However, his personality might have to explore different frequencies than the soul's original one, to integrate other aspects of life. Thus an individual will accomplish or experience other rays or vibrations, temporarily expressed then released.

GENETIC FACTORS

The genes of humankind have been re-engineered, crossed, altered on multiple occasions by extra-terrestrial beings and consciousnesses with or without selfish motives, with or without the authorization of the loving team of the Light. An easy example to clarify our thoughts: the Sirians, with the agreement of the Light Confederation, changed the humans' genes. The race was also altered by what we call greys. But, ultimately, where/what is the Light and where/what is the shadow? Aren't the Light and the Shadow working 'de concert'? All of life's unfoldment is still God moving through the universes.

In conclusion, you have to work and clear yourself in order to be as close as possible to your soul and then your Monad. Thus you become, step by step, the pure expression of the soul and the monad.

In the previous chapters, we invited you to retrieve the spiritual family that you belong to. Although your curiosity and independence led you to forget/abandon your true raison d'être, you each have a specific place in the Universal puzzle. Millions of years ago you were launched out of one creator's womb. This creator, plays on a vast chessboard, induces events or incidents that all unite into a particular plan. If you are/were supposed to intermingle, fuse to other frequencies, your creator will make sure to give you the right earthly families, according to the need of the story you are involved in. Some souls, especially those who have already achieved a high level of communication and consciousness are specially watched, trained, directed, supported to refine a ray, a specific quality of vibration. These souls are the keepers of the lineage of a creator.

When it is time for Spirit, via the creators, to manifest itself in the third dimension, the beings whose level of consciousness is ready then REMEMBER THEIR FILIATION. Suddenly, they might start channeling a Master or a group-the Melchizedeks for example, or an angel. The initiates will sometimes feel the filiation so deeply that they will be compelled to change their name and to utilize the creator's own name or the name of a Master. In some cases, a being might ask you precisely to change your name.

The creators are thus projecting themselves out to the third dimension, through their children, while the progenies, because of their evolution, stand in ecstasy, reaching out to Heaven and to the heart of Spirit. Literally, SPIRIT REJOINS MATTER, THE PURPOSE OF SPIRIT MANIFESTS THOUGH FUSION.

A group of individuals, or pioneers is now emerging. They are not just a frequency, a son of a specific lineage or aspect of a creator. They were born with a contract, signed with a great Being, to become, be an EMBODIMENT of this creator in the physical dimension, to open the doors to mankind.

A Spiritual Consciousness, pure Spirit, cannot incarnate without altering its power and essence. Nevertheless, Spirit has to be represented to anchor its frequency on earth on the path of sacralization. A spiritual entity might choose one, several bodies that he/she will form, train and utilize to represent, to extend him/herself, as a materialization on the physical dimension.

God, the Universal Consciousness, is descending and expending Itself through his creation, through each and every part of you. In a synergetic, consensual movement, Spirit and Matter, God and his creation are sparking the fire of Love, marriage and completeness.

Be Heaven on Earth, as it is God's heart/mind desire.

DISCUSSION WITH LORD MICHAEL

WHAT IS AN EMBODIMENT

An embodiment is the result of two or several aspects of the Divine Consciousness working concomitantly, as One. It is the natural consequence of remembering/re-membering, gathering the different aspects of the self, of Heaven and Earth coming together, of the fusion of several dimensions, of Oneness.

Here is an extract of the book "Jewel in the lotus" by Dr. Douglas Baker: "The Monad is a fragment of the flame like form of the Solar Logos which underlies and inter-penetrates His outer form. It is an indivisible fragment of Him, a Spark of the Divine."

A Logos, in order to be complete, like a human being, is (has) to know and integrate the entire scale of the vibrations of his domain.

God, Himself, extended His presence and re-produced Himself in the manifested creation. In order to simplify, we will use the image of a circle or a sphere.

In the center of the circle or sphere, is a living consciousness, whether a God, a Logos, a Monad, a soul. Whatever level of consciousness it is, its extension will move in all directions. A complete consciousness embraces the light and the shadow. More exactly, there is no limitation or differences but a fusion of all the dimensions or range of frequencies.

In the past, only a certain level of the Celestial Beings could reach the planet. This extension was achieved through the souls. Because of the immense work performed by both the spiritual planes and the human family, the Solar Logos is now ready to send Monads, pieces of Himself on Earth and human individual are prepared to receive them.

******

[Before receiving this message, during the day, I had a vision of Archangel Michael and felt his presence anchoring itself stronger and deeper in this body.]

An EMBODIMENT is an externalization, a crystallization of my essence, projected outside of myself, and organized as a hologram. Coming out of my being, in what would be the Hara, imagine a ray. Then a second one, a projection out of the symbolic 3rd eye of my Being.

Those two rays unite to form a materialization. This externalization is to carry my own divine principle, my own special attributes, and many of, let us say, my personality traits. Then, when the time has come, from my heart, another ray is sent to contact this part of myself, you, and imprint you, to add the influx, the essence of the Infinite Consciousness, Love.

EMBODIMENT

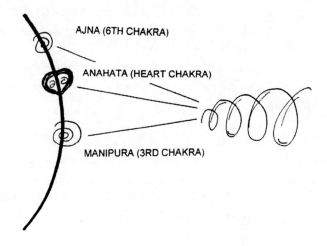

It is in fact my Love, joined with your openness of heart that gave life to this new aspect of you. Or, more precisely, re-enliven it, because, as you know, Beloved, we have been working together for eons, and you have been seeing my colors and calling me for many years, isn't it true Dear One?

Then, in the process of re-creation of myself through you, takes place an immense restructuring of your energy system. This process, Dear One, does affect your physical body and this is what you sometimes feel as tiredness. Be aware, Dear One, that Myself and many Masters are with you, assisting in this great change and rejoicing in the process. A soul is ready, another one, to carry the colors of God on the planet, in mission with us, the Universe Orchestra and in Perfect Oneness.

Be patient Dear One, we are watching and loving you. Your cries and tears are just remains of the past. Do not be hard on yourself. You are doing so well. We honor and cherish you. Keep practicing your listening skills.

With much Love and Honor. I AM MICHAEL. I AM your brother. Be strong. In Oneness. SO BE IT. NOW.

******

STORY

Below is the narration of one step of the process of embodiment, very incomplete and imperfect, because (it is) translated into human words excerpted from of a personal letter to Archangel Gabriel.

"Greetings to my Sister, the woman Gabriella
Greetings to my Brother, the Archangel

What a night! "You probably called around 1 am, this explains the difficulty I had to speak clearly immediately...

It is extra-ordinary to feel a little more each day Lord Michael/ my essence anchoring himself/itself more deeply and exteriorizing himself more naturally. Last night, after our conversation, we stayed together, us two or us four! I do not know if you were aware of what happened. My recollection of the details is vague, now, but you were at my side, and I was describing to you the process that I was experiencing, a fusion with Lord Michael, more physical, let us say.

I was feeling and seeing my body, my complete structure as well as my human cells undergoing contortions under the pressure of the ONE, of the multi-dimensions and of the fusion with the Archangel, that I AM. I would feel, observe and experience a process of melting/ merging/moving in all directions/dimensions at once. During this process, Lord Michael and Michael, my physical self, although al- ready One, were exploring and integrating different aspects of the planetary and universes evolution and memories, such as the oceans, the mountains, the rocks, the cetaceans, the dolphins, etc.

Although time does not exist, it seems, if I explain the process in linear space, that our universal memories were re-enforced or re-membered and merged, with more amplitude: higher, lower, multi-directional, with an extended awareness. The merging lasted several human hours.

I think that it was/is a way for Lord Michael to anchor himself more deeply in matter and for Michael, the physical vehicle, to con-sciously go higher (although none of these terms are exact!)."

At the time I am finishing this book, I have to say that, although I am still dealing with some aspects of the past, my health and ability to be happy dramatically improved. As soon as Michael took over and Nora left as an aspect of my ego, I mean overnight, I was healed of the heart trouble, that I had been experiencing for years. I had a light heart attack at 40 years old. Now, I am only tired at night. My cellular chemical balance is noticeably improved. I was already very sensitive, very empathic and sharing myself with others. I was already unable to ingest any chemical, homeopathic remedy or anything inappropriate without feeling an immediate reaction and often rejection. This sensitivity is exponentially increasing every day.

Also, my voice and tone are changing fast. My eyes did change immediately. The more I am following Lord Michael's and the I AM's instructions, the more blessings I receive. Ease and bliss are becoming part of my daily experience.

OVERSOUL

Several months before this discussion with Lord Michael, at the time of soul expansion and the merging with the I Am, I was working on a painting, on which two beings are inter-acting. One is the part of myself who was known as Nora and the second is my Monad with an aspect of Archangel Michael. Without really understanding why, at this time, I called this painting OVERSOUL.

Lord Michael:

Oversoul is a very difficult matter to understand for one who is still living in the 3rd dimensional world, as it has to do with multiple dimensions and realities being merged to function as one and yet individually.

When a being is coming from a filiation or a creator in need of forces to represent him/her, the celestial being might use a human or a "not-human" as an antenna or an instrument carrying his frequency, his capacities, his mission. In fact, because we are one, we are just all extensions of the Infinite Consciousness. In this regard, we are just facets, of the same Whole. One can then be a soul and yet have his own individuality, color, blue print. I, as Michael, have my own mission, responsibility in the vastness of this universe and the universes. I, then, have a number of beings, colored with my frequency and holding part of my blue print, according to the specific way they will be working and representing me. Nevertheless, some individual souls made a commitment with me to represent me in a very specific way. It is a matter of accepting to let go, very early, of the personal ego and merge more rapidly than others would normally do with the One Consciousness and my blue print. In your case, it is also, that we have been working "de concert" for years. Which means, that this body is trained to receive my frequency, manifest it, transmute it (make it accessible to humans in the physical dimension). This body, nervous system, brain are accustomed to flying in specific areas and dimensions where I need to be, in order to carry my purpose. It is then easier for us. Also, this body carries enough understanding, memories, intellectual background to follow my work and understand the telepathic information that I might have to transmit to him/her.

Let us say that those two souls or group souls-mine which is far from being describable to your human understanding and comprehension, limited by the screen of matter-and Nora-Michael's were working on the same matters, at different levels of frequencies. Remember that any action on earth has an effect on the subtle planes and vice versa. When you were operating in an area of the earth, on the physical plane or the astral, it would support our transformation of the general configuration of the blue print of these universes, in reference to the atomic placement of the light. In the other way, when I would think or initiate an action through the universes, regarding the lightning with the blue ray or the transmutation of the veils of death, or the DNA matrix carried through the different levels of 'matter' up to earth, Nora-Michael would translate that as an action in a group or a specific human area.

We, your oldest Brothers, as said in a linear way, are now even closer to earth. The recent changes in the planet made our coming to you easier. We are now walking, let us say, with our feet more on the ground, and anchoring Ourselves better every day. That is why, Dear One, I thank you for your efforts and still ask you with immense love and affection to please trust, stop the despair pattern and accompany us. Your decisions, stated yesterday and today are wonderful. Do your best; do not be too harsh on yourself. It is true that I need you Now. It is a little late, but we will catch up, because you can carry so much.

An oversoul is a soul who is overshadowing another one/group. They are going as one, in a common direction. The underlying frequency is one, unique although the coloring or externalization, expression might be different according to the specific area in which each of the members of the group is working. A being, an Archangel in this case, is overshadowing a portion of the many beings who are to work the ray or frequency that he carries. However even stated like that it is not completely accurate. Let us say that the more a vibration descends and scatters in the universes, the more difficult it is to keep it pure and formally made out of light and love. The waves are encountering what we could call obstacles, which are just screens, parts of realities that will interfere, and in fact, modify the original vibration. The instruments receiving this vibration or message will translate it according to their own blue print and within their own dimension or level of frequency. Can you imagine? It is the same thing as if trying to explain God's infinity, His Divine Holy Spirit, Wholeness, as well as his infinite diversity and yet, perfect Oneness.

Beloved, you are in my heart. Be blessed. Please, take care of the children. My love is pouring to you as your support. There is nothing to worry about. Aren't we Lord Michael? I Am the Lord of the Blue Ray. I Am Michael. I AM THAT I AM.

******

REHABILITATION OF THE DIVINE STATE

For millenniums, human beings have been conditioned to seek God outside of themselves. In the Judeo-Christian society, in particular, heaven is considered unfathomable, a magic, mystic, unrevealed land. The mystics, the ones in love of God, in perpetual ecstasy, are represented with their eyes turned towards the horizon or heaven. God is represented as such a powerful, dissimilar character that he is inaccessible and that prayer itself has rules.

All of these traits, which are common to a number of religions, are the consequence of the feeling of SEPARATION and reinforce separation. ORIGINAL SIN is not the disobedience of a rule decreed by a pseudo-human legislator. Original sin is instead, the temporary inability, imputable to physicality to see, feel, BE GOD, that is to say, TO LIVE your DIVINE NATURE.

You are not born out of God's womb, as a sinner. Sparks or parts of the unique diamond, vivified by Universal Spirit, divineness was offered as a birthright, a legacy. But you have forgotten. In your desire to discover the world, to be independent, a feeling that you might call freedom, you have lost the sense of your filiation. You have forgotten what you are, deep inside, by paternal filiation, a God, in the image of God, Sovereign of the terrestrial Kingdom that you create, co-creators of great universes.

It is this feeling, this innate and natural right that you must restore. However, speaking or envisioning this fact as a hope or philosophic context is not enough. You are asked to reach the God frequency, the Union with the Whole, to re-conquer Divineness. Beyond the words, beyond transcendental experiences, the candidate to the kingdom, once, feels the change so deeply in his cells, his body, his heart, that doubts are abolished. He is DIVINE, ONE, ETERNAL, GOD.

In the eyes of those who have not yet felt the STATE of BEING, those words are sometimes resented as blasphemous. Jesus Christ himself is still the center of political and religious discussions. The churches, the mystery schools are divided about the dogma of the divinity of Christ, the reality of his passage on earth and his sacrificial death. Because their discourse is not about what is really at stake. It is not about comprehending if Christ is the Infinite Consciousness, and vice-versa. It is difficult to imagine the Infinite Consciousness momentarily withdrawing itself in totality and moving into a unique human temple, tri-dimensional, in this case, Jesus' body. The Universes, deprived of the flow of life would have ceased to breathe while God was on Earth, preaching a new philosophy.

We realize how narrow, confining the words are, creating limits. The word God has been misused, diluted to the point of being inappropriate sometimes in our discourse. What we made of God, through religious interpretations, might prevent us from using this word as soon when we discover the splendor, the immensity of the Universal Consciousness. Great Architect of the Universe, Creator God. We personally like the expressions ALL IN ONE, INFINITE CONSCIOUSNESS. Or we use god, with a lower-case for spiritual beings, Co-Creators, the gods of Antiquity, and God, with a capital, for the Infinite Consciousness.

The names utilized in the religions, the sects, the mystery schools, the Kabbalah are only qualities, aspects of the ONE, of the DIVINE, corresponding to the needs of the races or groups. We respect and honor all these groups as instruments leading the sincere seeker, or appeasing his thirst, in the moment.

Prophets, religious or philosophical leaders all have a role to play in history. The Whole gave rise to their existence in order for the group consciousness to evolve in a precise direction.

Through multiple incarnations and inter-dimensional experiences, we approach the soul and the Whole, by way of various paths in resonance with our personal note, at a point in space/time. But this note is still a fragment of our symphony and not the totality of the Divine Consciousness. The self-sincerity and self-compassion of the seeker guide him to self-realization and to accept with joy these times, during which he sublimed and adored those fragments or aspects of the ALL IN ONE. At these times, the seeker was in harmony with certain facets of the diamond, he refined them and transformed them in Light, then in Conscious Light, the Light illuminated by the darkness, the fused Light.

It is the human interpretation that modifies the message, the simple message sent by God. Again, nobody is to be blamed, neither the prophet who received the communication, at his own level of awareness, nor the devotees who followed him. Everything in the universe is perfect and the flow of Love Consciousness is inexorably outpouring whether or not we understand its path.

CHRIST SHOWED THE PATH

CHRIST REALITY

Let us go back to the presence of the Christ. First there is no reality but the one that we perceive. Matter and life down here, only exist in our consciousness, and is yet an illusion. The world around us is only the reflection of our thoughts and feelings. Group consciousness, several times during the human journey, has been infused by exterior interventions. These events were set to trigger a shock, which would alter our level of consciousness and to give a new direction to humankind.

The presence of the Christ on earth was one of these propellings sent by our elder brothers or collective Higher Self. It served the planet in many ways:

CHANGE OF THE PLANETARY VIBRATIONS

The public life of the Nazarene and the incarnation of the Spiritual Being called Christ in Jesus' body obviously projected on earth an unusual vibration. This frequency touched all those who approached the Christ but also changed the aura of the planet. A seed was planted, the Christ Consciousness, which had to mature and blossom in order to finally hit a great number of souls. This is NOW occurring, it is the BIRTHING of the BODY of the CHRIST.

CHRIST AS AN EXAMPLE

The experience lived by Jesus is showing us the way. The man Jesus was taught by the Essenes and probably received the initiations available through this group. When he was ready, he presented himself to John the Baptist and received the Christic initiation, symbolized by the Dove. Through his baptism, he showed his desire to let go of the past and serve the Father, who recognized him: "This is my Beloved Son in whom I am well pleased." (Matt. 3,17)

Let us speak in the present, so that you can situate yourself and integrate the feeling involved in this story:

Jesus, now Jesus Christ accomplishes this ministry and is a living embodiment of divine mastery and the power of love. He performs miracles and heals. The message is: humans are much more than they think, they are in the image of God, they are divine.

Finally, he surrenders completely. Abdicating his own will to God's purpose, he spends three days in the kingdom of Death and resuscitates. The teachings: we have to abandon our so-called rights and surrender to the Creator in order to defeat death and move to spiritual consciousness—or for our time frame, to move to a new dimension, ascension or resurrection, depending on the situation.

YOU ARE THE ASCENDED MASTERS

An extraordinary phenomenon is taking place world wide before your eyes. Initiates from all nations have reached the required level of consciousness and purity to start merging with Heaven. Your oldest brothers, The Ascended Masters, are residing in the sixth and seventh dimensions. These great beings, experienced the same journey as yours and evolved to the point of leaving the physical world. If you bear in mind, the fact that we are all one, you easily understand that the Masters are a part of yourself, your Higher Self. Your joy and responsibility is then to connect yourself with them in such a tangible way that you feel yourself as an extension of the Masters, in the physical dimension.

I repeat, because it is important for you to integrate this message: "YOU ARE THE MASTERS" means:
1. You are simply asked to remember your origin, God's womb and to ACCEPT it as a fact and a tangible FEELING. It is necessary to be touched at two levels: comprehension/mind-and feelings/heart. You are divine and you are a Master. All the knowledge, all the tools are within you. Trust, be self-confident and you will remember. Act

-ELRO

every day as the Master that you are and this part of you will be more obvious, active, preponderant every day.

2. You are the extension of the Ascended Masters. They are your HIGHER SELF, they are YOU. Recognize and integrate this idea. Then, integrate it into your daily life and you will accomplish your mission. Your mission is to MANIFEST, TO BE THE MASTERS, the HIERARCHIES, GOD, what you already ARE.

******

BELOVED READERS

What can be written about God, when God is essentially felt, as a STATE, an EMOTION?

I closed my eyes, and felt God in my chest, in my heart, and then GOD everywhere. Well, I must bring this to a very human level to transfer that concept. It was champagne, champagne in my body. Sparkles of life, laughing and bubbling, in unison. Sparks of life, ascending to touch heaven, to touch spirit, to BE SPIRIT.

And this sweet, strong, marvelous, fulfilling sensation of ONE-NESS, JOY, GRATITUDE, LOVE. The feeling of home. No more questions, no more searching, no more needs, nothing but the immensity of the reconciled SELF. No more separation, just one immense heart, one emotion.

I wrote about my experience, my thoughts, how to connect with your creator and then to your DIVINE PRESENCE, but nothing, nothing beloved, can convey the feeling, the emotion, whose root is in total, unconditional let go and surrender. MAY YOU FIND THAT on your path, in your heart. May you BE THAT ceaselessly. Experience it as many times as possible during your day, before going to sleep AND THEN, be it, BE GOD.

SECTION IV

LACK OF INTEGRATION

Although you now have to extend your belief system to the point of integrated realities that have nothing to do with the present world, it is still critical to deal, in the moment, with the world as it is. A serious problem is unfortunately affecting the disciples, who often hesitate to position themselves in the third or fourth dimension. The immediate result is a separation between the level of awareness and consciousness achieved on the spiritual planes and the life in the physical body.

We are happy to observe and work with more and more Masters in the physical world who have initiated a strong connection with their soul, with Father/Mother God. Those beautiful beings are serving in integrity, preparing themselves for ascension, integrating the Divine. However, they are still dealing with the old self, the ego, facing a dissonant personality, the patterns of the old self, living the earthly life in poverty.

You are all Masters Beloved Ones, but it is also your duty, in order to reach full Godness, to bring mastery in the Third dimension. That is to say to balance the different aspects of the self without neglecting Mastery of the third dimension, because you are too much involved and concentrated on spiritual matters.

A strong emphasis was made during the past decades by the Ascended Masters and the spiritual teachers to guide as many workers as possible on the path of enlightenment and initiation. The goal was to connect them with their spiritual self. The human family has

Been blessed and successful. But, Beloved, it is now time to anchor your whole self on the planet, in order to bring the divine frequency on Earth and participate in the transmutation of the Mother. Ascension has to be balanced by descension. The six-pointed star is complete when Spirit meets Matter, that is to say when balance of the forces is established. Matter has to be spiritualized while Spirit is manifested through form.

We are not advocating that the third dimensional world is either paradise, or the promised Kingdom. We are not forgetting the lack of compassion, the injustice, the pain still affecting humankind. We are not praising money and power as important. However:

-Feelings are negative and painful only because of your point of view, your attachment and your preconceived ideas or judgements.

-Money, power and sex are the remains of a dimension, a consequence of survival and fear, but still ruling part of your existence.

-As long as you do not exit completely and definitely the game, or the movie of the third dimension, your goal is to balance all the aspects of the Self, physical, emotional, mental and spiritual. At the very minute that you master these frequencies (fear, survival, money, sex and power) they cease to exist, that is to say to have any impact in your existence.

Finally, bear in mind that the spiritual planes as well as the spiritual beings are descending towards you, integrating fully within themselves the physical dimension. This is the true significance of a total merging of Heaven and Earth. Consequently, it is your duty, Dear Ones, to assume the responsibility that you signed up for, that is to say, be born and master the third dimension:

It is your assignment to honor and take care of your body as God's temple, as an extraordinary tool, in which you are to discover the pleasures and vicissitudes associated with matter. Would you despise God's gift? Certainly not. Then you are expected to feed this body with balanced food, to be clean, to heal yourself if necessary, and to provide yourself with a home.

Of course, if you choose to live in the woods, build a hut and practice shamanic arts, so be it. But if you have a family, we would remind you that their presence in your life is a blessing and supporting them emotionally and financially is an expression of your love. Although, we believe that more and more people will live in communities and share their gifts, this is still for the future.

It is true that in the ancient civilizations or in native tribes, still close to nature and to God, seniors, priests, artists, healers were/are honored and taken care of. Today, a number of disciples want to support themselves in the field of metaphysics but are unable to face their financial responsibilities. Although we speak out of our heart, in full compassion and non-judgement, we are asking you to question yourselves: what is your blueprint? Is there any earthy activity that you could practice to support yourself, still feel happy and in alignment with your light? Have you examined your life in prayer and divine consciousness? Are you a healer because you are not healed yet? Or are you teaching yoga because your energy system is incomplete? Are you teaching because you are still looking for your truth? There are many paths, many occupations through which you can help the community and heal the world. Also, do not forget that true Masters mainly work on the subtle planes, inter-dimensionally, and in silence.

In conclusion, although you have to surrender and live in the present, please be balanced and clear in regards to your incarnation of the Presence.

WHY ARE THE DISCIPLES ONLY EVOLVING SPIRITUALLY?

1. BECAUSE INCARNATION IS ASSOCIATED WITH PAIN

Do not beat yourself up, it is an acquired reflex! Being in the body, participating in the third dimension is, subconsciously, a source of challenges, heaviness and even problems. You have been entertaining the idea that paradise is out of the planet, eventually accessible after your death or without a physical body. You are on earth to suffer, to do penance, and you have had a lot of experiences to accredit these beliefs.

Nevertheless, while you are growing spiritually, the comprehension of universal laws, the acquisition of wisdom as well as your love for others are healing the layers of memories left in you from the third dimension, based on transmuted assessments and thoughts. Your focus is now on creating a new life, clear and simple. If you believe in your Godness, and thus in the infinite possibilities of the Universe, if you trust and surrender to the unknown, then you will co-create a new life, a new world for yourself and for others.

The disciple must accept this process as a possibility, open himself to heal, harmoniously, all the layers of his personality, his structure. He has to become conscious of the significance of the body and of life in matter:

-Acknowledgment and gratitude for the incarnation
-Acceptance to live one's life fully, in the now.
-Externalization of one's love for life, expressed through joy
-Actions demonstrating that you are grounded, take your responsibilities in the terrestrial tasks.
-Clearing of any code, mental process or belief system responsible for non-integration or survival mode, instead of enjoying life, now.

2. THE INCARNATION IS ASSOCIATED WITH SIN AND SHADOW

This belief is also part of your cellular memories. In order to reach freedom and truth, to center yourself in perfection and divineness, you need to perform a gigantic cleansing. The remembering of your glorious destiny is still present in your soul, but the contact is intermittent, and you are still guided by the deceptive memories of the past.

Most human beings have been damaged by the theories about sin and the devil. Many advanced disciples still have an unclear definition and comprehension about the two sides of the energy and about the shadow. They are reticent or frightened at the idea of engaging themselves on the purification path in the kingdom of the darkness. It is now time, for all of you, Beloved light worker, to be reconciled with the phenomenon of duality and the multiple aspects of creation. Nothing, Dear Ones, nothing is imperfect, nothing is shameful. Everything, everyone carrying God's divine life force is divine. There is no such a thing as a demon, a Satan, as defined by Christian churches. There is only God, Father/mother God, Whole, One, and the Self. Anything outside of Self is a creation by Self. There is no threat, no enemy, no darkness, but thoughts and questions emitted by Self.

The only sin, if such a concept even existed, would be, for the self to choose, in full responsibility or consciousness:
A. To act or practice something that you know as contrary to the law of universal love.
-I know that stealing my friend's mate will create hurt, but I persist.
-I use my physical strength or situation of power to hurt others
   physically or emotionally
-I lie to myself or to others, thinking that nobody will ever discover
   the truth.

B. Act against your spiritual consciousness or your I AM Presence, or the piece of Universal Consciousness that is seeded within you.
When you start to grow spiritually, you do not need anyone to explain to you the divine laws and the significance of unconditional love. You feel good and evil in your heart. Then do you obey or are you resisting?

3. PRESSURE OF THE SPIRIT

For centuries, and because of the necessity of establishing a higher level of consciousness for the planet and humankind, the Hierarchy and its leaders pushed the disciples upwards, toward Spirit. The accent was set on the importance of letting go of the energies connected with the inferior chakras, and purifying the shadow. You were encouraged to open and work mostly with the centers in the head, to meditate as often as possible and to seek contact with the spiritual realms.

4. RUNNING AWAY FROM RESPONSIBILITIES

It is often much easier to live with your pain, challenges, unconsciousness than to accept looking at yourself in a mirror and to change. There are two categories of individuals:

-Those who have access to their souls, know who they are and what is to be transmuted, but have no courage to do it, because of fear or tiredness. To these Beloved Ones, our message is:

"Beloved, we love you deeply and honor God in you. We are all brothers, united in service. We honor your pain and difficulties and pray, with you, so that you will find the strength to harmonize yourself with the desire of your soul and of your heart. Remember the words of Christ: "Put your burden on me". Invoke the Christ, who manifested God in the flesh. Invoke your Monad, your I AM Presence, so that it will take charge of your life. Stop judging yourself, diminishing yourself, stepping into fear and misery. Love yourself before trying to love others. Love yourself as an extension of the Creator God. Would you dare to judge God?

We salute you and love you unconditionally.
I AM MICHAEL

-Those who have completely forgotten, lost contact with their soul and might not be reading this book. The conscious brothers/sisters are then responsible. We are a unique body, and if one of the organs is sick, the healthy ones are taking over, aren't they? Yes, because of fear, habit, passion, a fraction of God's children sank in matter to the point that they do not hear the messages of the soul, or hear so briefly, that they do not pay attention.

However, as a unique body, all mankind is gloriously progressing. Many are receiving the influx of the light workers, the planet and the cosmic Hierarchies. One day they will hear the call, in the body. The disciples and initiates have to manifest patience, compassion and to remember that they are the pioneers, the bringers of the Christ frequency. They are blessed and have to BE, without judgement.

5. MEMORY OF MONASTIC LIFE

Many disciples carry in their memories the experience of life in a monastery, a church with strict rules, a time when enjoying life, sexuality, aesthetics or wealth was neither accessible to the majority, nor acceptable to the mystic or the sincere believer.

6. OLD SOULS

It is often more difficult for a powerful being, who is accustomed to manipulating energies and thinking that he is in control of his life to manifest. Why?

Old souls, you for whom magic is a routine, have to let go of the magician, of the habit of control. Lines of forces that you have created often surround you. These magnetic lines are an exteriorized image of your internal geometry, and might reflect your complexity or difficulties. This might result in a short-circuit. I recommend for you, the magicians, to follow the channels of the vital force, on your own structure and to clear them from any etherical and astral miasms that are not in harmony with your immediate purpose. These residues might be:
-Implants and entities
-Residues of contracts and rituals
-Thought forms

Do not stay locked, focused on your challenges. Do not judge yourself. Use your lessons as stepping stones, as a mirror. Correct what you can and give the rest to God. He will take on the burden.

Light Workers are pioneers. Between two eras, "walking between the worlds", they are preparing, opening the path for humankind, discovering, experimenting new ways, new laws. They are changing, implanting those new frequencies within themselves and facilitating the re-patterning of others. Beloved workers, consider this as a great honor. God trusts you and collaborates with you in his magnificent scheme. You are fully loved and supported.

Although the initiate might not be directly responsible for the presence of these residues or beings, we will add that devas, elementals entities, attracted by the power of old souls, escort you. They read your mind or listen to what you are announcing like facts, and then, have the pleasure of manifesting it for you. The devas' and elementals' minds are not ill-intentioned, but they are much simpler than you are, just like Aladdin's genie. You ask for a pumpkin and you get a pumpkin. You order one ton of chewing gum and you receive it on your head. If you have forgotten to give the size of the pumpkin or the address of the warehouse for the candies, you might be surprised.

Below are the principles of manifestation, from two points of view, from the third and the fourth dimension.

THIRD DIMENSION:
-Develop the ability to create from your brain/energy
Increase your energy/power
Focus
Clarity of self and of intent
Let go
FOURTH DIMENSION:
-Setting the environment (you)
Let go of doubt, improve faith
Self-recognition, self love

Clear the subconscious mind of any desires
Recognize what you have already accomplished
Surrender

-Group or collective principles
Alignment and acceptance of the group
Understanding that the group, expressing itself within the universe
is subject to the right timing
Surrender to the flow, to conjunctions of energies

FIFTH DIMENSION
Manifestation is no longer a personal matter, but the alignment
with the group, group consciousness, God's purpose.
-Unconditional love
-Unconditional surrender to God
-ONENESS
-BEING GOD.

The quality of the relationship existing between the disciple and
God is still veiled by the presence of the ego and the habit of counting
solely on the self. If there is a blockage, think about these principles:

-The stronger the desire, the more one is projecting his will.
Be detached. Who is really going to benefit from the object of
your desire? How is it serving the community?

-The orientation of the intent, the vision is contrary to the initiate's
destiny or divine blueprint.

-There is a twist in the being's energy. Seek for alignment with
God and your Monad.
The being who merges himself, in humble but full awareness,
with the Monad, the heart of the Solar Logos, lets go of his ego, his
desires, his will and then surrenders completely. As One, he is in love
with God, for his Godself and he serves. Manifestation is no more a

question of personal power; it is a fusion with the highest part of the self, the Divine, in order to create perfection and HEAVEN ON EARTH.

******

FREE YOURSELF FROM THE PAST

In order to embrace fully the path of the Christ and the Christ Consciousness, you have to get rid of any habit, any belief inherent to the past. The system, in which we are shifting, has nothing to do with what you might know or imagine. Moral or religious beliefs, relationships, sex, marriage, medicine and health, family, work, everything is under deep modifications. Nobody really knows God's mind and plan for the next few years. Religions, philosophies, customs are human creations, connected with the third dimensional world. All of this is in the process of being abolished for the immensity, diversity, bliss of unconditional love, that is the foundation of Gods' personality, if we can use such words!

So, beloved, we are asking you, expressly, to become immune to others decisions, behavior, philosophies. Stay joyous, strong and your own evolution and integration process of Heaven on Earth will be a success, a source of blessings, NOW.

KEEP YOURSELF CENTERED IN THE DIVINE WAY

Start the day, pledging allegiance to the All Pervading God, your All Mighty I AM Presence, (and to Archangel Michael, in my own case).

Repeat out loud your unconditional love for God, the Universal Consciousness, the Ascended Masters or Beings that you feel comfortable/connected with, the Christ.

Repeat your heart desire-this is to be truly felt—to serve the Cosmic and planetary Hierarchies, to serve planet Earth, to serve your beloved brothers and sisters, on the subtle planes but primarily on the physical plane.

Plan and make a habit of accomplishing any task, as if you were asked to do it by God and for God Him/Herself or a heavenly Master. The daily chores, cleaning, filing, are an excellent exercise to train your mind. Accomplish it in a meditative state. Do not allow your mind to wander, especially on the past, on your difficulties, your health or anything that is not pure love, pure harmony and pure beauty. Each time you feel a strain in doing something, for instance cleaning the bathroom or picking up a paper, center yourself in the pure love frequency and say out loud: "I do it as a service to others and to the planet, I do it in love, this is an expression of Love", and feel it.

If you have a hard time quieting the mind, choose to chant, tone or to repeat mantras. The mantras will depend on what you are wishing to achieve in the moment. Repeating the names of your Beloved older Brothers or for some the names of God. Feel free to adapt your spiritual exercises with your own core pattern, what you feel you are, or what resonates with you because of your education or your childhood. Still, we would recommend that you re-examine your choices frequently and ask yourself if you are operating in attunement with the now, your I Am Presence or still because of what you were taught by your parents, a church or a more recent guru/teacher.

As stated before by a number of writers, most of our thoughts are either remembrances about the past, past events, past conversations with our friends, relatives, colleagues, or projections of our mental patterns into the future. When we think about the future, are we projecting paradisiacal thoughts of love and bliss or are we dwelling on old unresolved problems?

Each time that you find yourself thinking, stop, cancel or transmute the thought according to divine philosophy, center yourself in the heart and put yourself in "position Christ":

By "position Christ" we mean broadcaster of love, wisdom and light, centered at least in the 5th dimension, without judgement and in the now. Your mind is silent, you are radiant, you serve God and mankind with deep respect. You humbly surrender to the All In One's will, to the Universe, to God. You are a pure and unconditional channel for the Light and Divine Love.

I suggest, if this feels right for you, to visualize yourself with christic traits, features, with the face and feeling of the Christ, your arms open as a symbol of self-offering and service. You can use this image as a symbol to anchor yourself quickly in the christic frequency and re-harmonize yourself any time that you slip into the intricacies and dramas of the subconscious mind.

SECTION V

TECHNIQUES

The techniques proposed in this section are applicable to everyone, but easier to apply and more efficient for the students who already:
-Faced most of their emotional challenges
-Fairly developed their chakra system
-Opened the upper chakras to allow free communication with the spiritual planes
-Established a permanent contact with the soul

BEGINNERS

For those who do not practice regularly, we would recommend for them practice the techniques offered in the manual I AM THAT I AM, ALTA MAJOR. It is advised to read and work with chapter One, Section II and 3, Section IV.

BEFORE ANY EXERCISE

Before using any technique, be comfortably seated in a lotus position or in a chair. If you are using a chair, keep your feet flat on the ground, without crossing your legs.

Breathe deeply through the nose, from your abdomen. In order to practice abdominal breathing, place one hand on your lower abdomen and inhale deeply, through the nose, feeling the air expanding your abdomen. Make sure to push the air into the lower abdomen and not only into the lungs. Then, exhale slowly, through the nose. Repeat three to seven times. Focusing on the breath induces a relaxed state for your body and opens the energy channels.

SETTING YOUR INTENT

While starting any spiritual technique, announce out loud and clearly your intent, for instance:

"I am . . . , I am Divine

I, . . . , as a soul and as a human being, am working today on . . . my left eye, blood circulation, on the problem that occurred at age 10.

Or: I desire to harmonize my chakras.

Be either very precise or perfectly surrendered to your Monad and to the God:

" I, . . . , as my Monad
And Divine I Am Presence
Collaborate in the healing of all the levels of my being
From the physical to the highest dimensions,
I align myself with God's perfection
And with my Divine blueprint
SO BE IT, NOW

Divine I Am Presence
Preside over my path, my actions, and my thoughts
I surrender to God

TONING

We are encouraging all seekers and readers to let go of self-judgement and to practice intuitive toning. Just trust yourself, you know what tones are appropriate, in the now. After some weeks of practice you might be amazed by the results.

Start with an Aum or with a lower tone that you feel comfortable with. Inhale deeply, through the nose and project the sound out while exhaling.

In order to make it easier and go beyond your shyness, you may start with a MMMM and add the vowel of your choice, for instance: MMMM . . . aaaa or MMMM . . . EEEE.

VISUALIZATION/MANIPULATION OF THE ENERGIES

When you feel ready, not only relaxed but in a shifted state of consciousness, start to build or shape your energies, using visualization and your will/intent. If you feel like it, you may also use your hands to position your energy or chakras. Whether or not you see or feel is not important. Act like it . . . and the ability will develop.

We are giving you several geometrical figures that you will visualize on/in you in order to add them to your structure and implant your genes. "On you" means that you see yourself sitting in the geometrical shape. "In you": you visualize the patterns imprinted in one cell, two cells, ten, and so on. Then you show your trust in yourself and ask your Higher Self to keep duplicating. Finally, you release your attention and surrender to the perfection of the universe-what is good for you is done.

I have applied all the techniques mentioned in my books. For more than twenty years, I have been sitting and asked: "what is the next step?" or "How to achieve . . . . ?" and was given the appropriate technique and sounds. Also, I have been observing, noticing the geometrical shapes being created and implanted in people while I was toning. I have chosen to gather the simplest, fastest, most effective techniques.

TRIANGLE—BALANCING THE EMOTIONAL BODY

This paragraph is excerpted from I AM THAT I AM. This technique is very fast for balancing your system. The beginners might also employ it, to start visualizing with an easy geometrical shape.

"This technique is to facilitate the integration of your emotional body and its alignment with the physical and spiritual layers. Located in the liver is the active essence of paternal heredity, written in the red blood cells. The spleen contains the maternal heritage, imprinted in the white cells. Father and mother are, of course, the symbols of the feminine and masculine energies, which must be balanced to achieve the raising up of the Kundalini.

EXERCISE:
-Assume a lotus position—or get as close to this position as you can.
-Breathe deeply, maintain a state of relaxation.
-Focus your attention on the Ajna (center of the forehead). See the Light, possibly even the colors associated with this center.
When you are able to see/grasp this chakra correctly, connect it to two different spots in your body:
* The liver, on the right side, with a golden bridge.
* The spleen, on your left, with a silver link.

In essence, you are building a triangle whose apex is the Ajna. Stabilize this triangle of Light for 10 minutes."

PENTAGRAM—FIVE POINTED STAR

The pentagram is found in many traditions. The number five represents life in the human body or third dimension. When you visualize a pentagram around you or in each of your cells, you balance yourself as living in a physical body, you harmonize your organs, functions before jumping to higher frequencies.

The five elements are the base of Chinese acupuncture, Tai Chi, Feng Shui, etc. When the energies of the organs and meridians are correctly and equally distributed in the body, you feel free and happy. Good health is the result of proper equilibrium of the forces or energies in your structures, including the:
-Physical level
-Emotional level
-Relationships with soul and monad
-Relationships with the cosmic system and the Beings composing it.

 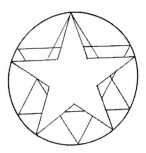

The next step is to visualize a six-pointed star on you. Your body has to fit in the image. The upper triangle reaches about one foot above your head.

OCTAHEDRON

This pattern tends to establish a complete equilibrium between Spirit and Matter and is very easy to visualize. The seeker accepts to be fully incarnated. He does not only pursue the mirage of spiritual, heavenly realization. He understands that he has to integrate all that HE IS, as a soul, a Monad and spiritual essence, in his Whole structure and therefore in his physical vehicle.

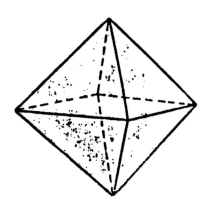

This technique stabilizes, introduces the soul, and then the Monad in the third dimension, into the daily activities. It helps to become conscious of what the Divine wants to express through you. You will know what and how to do, in the now.

Visualize yourself sitting in the center of an octahedron, and keep the picture clearly in your mind, as long as possible. After several minutes or seconds, according to your abilities, you will feel a shift in your vibratory rate. Not only will you be quiet and serene, but, also in an extended and divine state of consciousness, in complete balance.

This picture is extremely effective and easy to hold. More geometrical figures can be added, as suggested by many authors and speakers. However, I noticed that a lot of students have difficulties keeping sophisticated pictures in their mind. The octahedron is powerful enough to change your inner geometry.

****

On January the 19th, 1999, when the whale consciousness merged with planet earth, I noticed another very interesting flow of energy on/in myself, that can indeed be added to these techniques. It includes the pattern of the flower of life, taught by several beings, from the Melchizedek lineage. Below, I am again translating our experience into a technique:

Be seated comfortably and breathe as stated above.
Create a tube a light, going through your spine, 3 inches wide. The cylinder of light reaches Heaven through your crown chakra and your 'anchor to Spirit'. It is grounded in Matter, in the earth through your first center and your 'anchor to matter'. (See Duality).

The flow of fused energy, Heaven, Earth and Heart, stops in your heart to include the Christ Consciousness frequency. It is pink in color.

Then the bright pink energy flows out from the front and the back of the heart chakra. It creates a sphere all around you. This sphere is composed of pink petals, organized according to the pattern of the flower of life. Then the energy changes to a violet hue, that is to say that you are surrounded by a sphere of energy, constituted of violet petals, arranged according to the Flower of Life pattern.

ARCHANGEL MICHAEL'S POINT OF VIEW: THE UNIVERSAL TECHNIQUE

For years, you have been trying, experiencing, and inventing all kind of techniques. Breathing, meditation, yoga, visualization, etc. Each and all of them may contribute to correcting, transmuting, and aligning a little bit of yourself, especially if you would trust enough to work strictly on intuition. If you are looking for a method, a new way to learn, question clearly and wait. A book, a flyer might be handed to you. If you are offered a sensational technique, again, ask your Higher Self, about its origin and appropriateness.

Then, when you have found it, use it responsibly and with perseverance. But, Beloved, what is the best technique? Think about Christ, Mother Teresa. What were they doing? Surrender, detachment, service and Love.

The UNIVERSAL TECHNIQUE is the art of connecting yourself, as much as possible, with the universal life, within the heart of God, of the Infinite Consciousness. The most important words are, Unity, At-One-ment, Alignment, symbiosis, love.

If you can forget all about your life, let go of the past and center yourself on the Divine Consciousness; if you can get rid of any internal turmoil and debates, and only be nurtured by the vital force, by love, without obstruction, without judgement, without limitations, without personal thoughts; if you are ONE with the WHOLE, as often as possible, then you are ONE, you are WHOLE and COMPLETE.

You remembered, recovered your essence, in the NOW, out of space and out of time.

Dear Ones, we are proposing that you offer to yourself, whenever you feel like it, periods of REST. At these times, you will stop all techniques, any routine that you might almost be addicted to. Retire in SILENCE, in the silence of your own beauty and perfection. Connect yourself, your heart with God's heart. You might think about the words: "Knock and the door will open. Ask your Divine I AM Presence, the Cosmic Masters, your personal Angel, the Almighty Archangels, the Holy Spirit to collaborate in your purification and alignment with MOTHER/FATHER GOD.

The second part of this technique is SERVICE, SERVICE, and SERVICE. Serve your family, friends, students, employees, and community. A new society is emerging, based on trust, personal responsibility and unconditional love. May your behavior, your words, your actions be the reflection of the Presence. May each moment in your existence, on any planet or dimension be a praise to life, to beauty, to the others, to God. Be God's MANIFESTATION on planet Earth. What a joy, felicity, honor! Become, BE God manifested in the body.

CONCLUSION

CONCLUSION:
SECRET OF MANIFESTATION

Lord Michael, what is the secret of Manifestation?

Beloved, nothing in life is secret. Everything is elucidated, explained at the right moment. The laws of the universe are revealed to the seeker. It is not necessary to be a knowledgeable scientist to have access to the common sense or to the heart of God.

Aligning oneself with the heartbeat of God, what a plan. Well to start, you announce your wish to be in agreement, ONE with God's heart and its wondrous pulsation. Beloved, every morning and every night, before going to sleep, say out loud, claim your desire to be one with God's heart. Your words will seal your intent, and engage your responsibility.

When you align yourself with God's heart, you place yourself in the natural flow of Divine Love. Love is the key to any realization, relationship, manifestation, and abundance. It is the cement of the universe, the glue, and as you imagine, a very soft one.

When you center yourself in this flow, you recognize your position as a son/daughter of God. Has the Father ever abandoned his children? Did he fail to keep his promises? Only the child who made the decision, himself to leave the family to enjoy his own experiences is not completely taken care of by the Father. In this case, the Father will momentarily withdraw to express his paternal love through respect and freedom, so that the son may experience what he feels important. This is what humankind as a group wanted, but then, perceived as sorrow, the separation.

Knowing that the Father loves you engenders a feeling of joy, uninterrupted connection, trust in others, detachment about the future and capacity to enjoy the present. When one feels loved, he loves himself more and loves others. No more questions, doubts, lack of self-confidence, guilt, depression, addictions.

Feeling God's love illuminates the heart, face, cells. The divine flow penetrates the body, maintaining it in good health, harmonizing the physical vehicle with its daily needs. The awareness and feeling of God's love are the most powerful and exquisite food for the entire self. Centered in peace, the individual is perfectly healthy, emotionally and physically. He receives the vital force, filtered by Love. This energy is not only a source of strength but also provides all the nutrients, minerals, vitamins you require. Beloved I am proposing here serious competition to all doctors, health practitioners, nutritionists and health food stores!

Being with and in God's heart, you are, you reflect the greatest of God's attributes, to which nothing and nobody resists. Most of the resistance, negative emotions, hurts, solitude, divorces are the result of a lack of love, aren't they, or of a deformation of the original unselfish quality of Love. When one walks, speaks, is, radiant divine love, all the doors are open.

The satisfaction of selfish desires, competition, lack of humility, all these qualities of vibration vanish when a being is One with the heart of God. These fruits of the flesh, or manifestations of the third dimension are naturally replaced by the fruits of spirit, humility, grace, loving presence. Beloved, if you are those vibrations in your life, your friends and accomplishments will be countless. You will live in peace, joy, harmony and then abundance. Of course this word means the uninterrupted flow of everything that exists in the creation, the flow of blessings, joy, peace, harmony, beauty, love and abundance.

The secret of the secret is in the capacity to hear, to listen, to obey and to receive. Those who think that there might be a secret are those who did not cultivate silence, silence of the mind. In order to hear God's voice, one must be silent, because God certainly does not scream. Then, you still need to keep your ears open, and let the message enter the consciousness and blossom. When the divine Consciousness asks to do or not to do something, you must obey, whether or not you understand the message or the situation.

When one is finally and consciously connected with I AM, with the Monad, he also has more responsibilities. It is harmful then to argue or refuse to listen. That would mean to reject the support of the Universal Consciousness and then, to stand in a twisted relationship with the flow of life.

Beloved, I urge you to examine yourself, any time that your way becomes difficult, any time that you loose inner joy and harmony. Ask yourself: When did this start? When did I stop manifesting perfection? Did I ask a question or hear a message that I did not listen to? Did I refuse to follow my intuition about something or someone?

Then, as soon as you have found an answer, call God and your Monad, express your feelings, in pure simplicity, the reason why you did not listen. Beloved, you will immediately feel divine compassion and will love more. Ask for the support of your I AM Presence and of the Lord, so that you can commit and accomplish what you have been asked. Then, do not hesitate. OBEY and walk in peace.

God does not always speak directly, but He is everywhere, isn't He? In his compassion, God understands that some are not ready to hear his voice directly. Source might then use intermediaries to teach us how to listen and recognize him in the whole creation.

****

In stillness and perfect beauty,
From the harmony of heart and action
In the depth of serenity
Emerging from the reconciled Whole,
I project myself,
I taste life flowing
Soft and vibrant, strong and nestled
In the present moment

God is here, within me, me, so strong, so constant
No question, no challenges
The past has vanished in the distance
As old disembodied ghosts

Life swirls and dances in the womb of I AM
In the arms of the Lords and of the Universe.

Thank you for sharing yourself with us
With sweet compassion and much Love

I AM ARCHANGEL MICHAEL
I AM THAT I AM

BVG